NEARLY FINISHED

a guide to home renovation

ROBYN COHEN

DOUBLE STOREY
a juta company

This book is dedicated to my husband Greg (aka GTB, Greg the Builder)

Published 2006
by Double Storey Books,
a division of Juta & Co. Ltd,
Mercury Crescent, Wetton, Cape Town

ISBN-10: 1 77013 099 3
ISBN-13: 978 1 77013 099 9

Editing by Jacqui L'Ange
Text design and layout by Jenny Young
Cover design by Toby Newsome
Printing by Paarl Print, Paarl

Contents

Thank you

To Bridget Impey of Double Storey: it was your idea to do this book and you coined the title, which says it all. Thanks to Russell Martin (Double Storey), Toby Newsome (fab cover design), Jacqui L'Ange (editor) and Jenny Young (designer). To Jen Crocker, my commissioning editor at the Cape Times, thanks as always for your support, enthusiasm and invaluable input. Paul van der Spuy of Lateral Studio; Allison Foat (Diva Events, Marketing, Publicity) and Morice Wohlman (Memo Communications) and Errieda du Toit: you have all been fantastic.

Friends etc.

Thanks for cheering us along. Special mention to those who were frequent visitors to the site: Guy, who climbed on to the roof many times and gave moral support to GTB; Food Safety; Adi and Dan (who got into the swing with bling); Jeff and Enid; Gary and Janet; Fern; Audrey; Tanya (paint and handle correspondent); Barbara (kitchen confidante); Meg (storage mentor); Shawn and Belinda; Lynn; Janene and Paolo; Lorraine and Rael (TV/cable dingus man par excellence). Nthabiseng (Rebecca) – Rebs – thanks for the Xhosa and for putting up with the mess. And to the Joburg contingent: Josh; Saul, Mari and children; Michelle and Eric – thanks for everything.

Jessie and Sarah would like to thank

Laurie, Taz, Jessica, Mirandsky, Sam, Tamsin, Mika, Estee, Abigail, Arielle, Natasha, Yael, Kim and all their friends who braved the house of ruins and reminded them that homework had to be done … and teachers for being understanding about this renovating gig.

Neigbours for their patience

Roy, Paddy and Melanie; Raelene; Craig and Lisa; Shaun and Carmen.

Mommas and poppas

Mom, for all the support, laughs and supper parcels sent via priority post. Ann and Sam, for advice and emergency provisions when we really needed them.

Team building

The Cupido family, especially Charles (Snr) and his team, the best baksteen mense; Uncle Martin; Tony and Alfa; Roderick; Mike for his wonderful cupboards; Paul for landscaping under pressure; Andries, Willie, and each and every other person who helped – too numerous to name.

Home team

Greg, for your amazing knowledge of building and for taking us all on this magical mystery tour. To our darling daughters Jessie and Sarah for being terrific sports amidst the balagan. We really are Nearly Finished. Amper Klaar. Sekufutshane Ndiggibe.

How it **started**

This book is based on 'The Story of my House', a series of articles published in the *Cape Times* that elicited some rather interesting responses. 'My husband wants to renovate and I don't. Please compile a book of your building articles, so I can scare him off,' implored Desperate from Newlands. 'I missed the cupboard and paint article. Self-addressed envelope enclosed. Send. Reward offered,' from one reader. 'Please publish your hysterical, hilarious articles,' implored others.

Thanks a lot, glad you found them funny.

My brief was to write five or six articles documenting our house as it was ripped apart into a pile of ruins and then put back together. The articles were written from the perspective of – and pitched at – homeowners (ourselves) who were on a tight budget. To our delight, readers from all walks of life – including property developers, architects, designers, electricians, plumbers and individuals where money is no object – responded and asked for more.

Frustrated from Fresnaye called me at some ungodly hour in the morning, before the birds were singing. It sounded like a fun call initiated by a radio station. From my life as a hack, I have learnt never to presume anything. I listened politely while FF implored me to phone her architect and give him a message. No, I would not call the architect, I declined firmly. The architect duly called me later in the day. Why? Because his client told him to. I advised them to go for counselling.

Estate agents working in residential, commercial and industrial property sectors have been very enthusiastic respondents. They say that their clients are constantly asking if a bathroom can be swapped with a kitchen or if a wall can be bashed out.

A gentleman developer of high-rise buildings offered me a job as a 'plan-walker', as he put it. He offered to pay me good '*latkes*' (Yiddish speak for cash) to walk his plans through local council.

I was surprised. Surely anyone embarking on a million-rand project would employ a project manager to advise on these details? It seems that even with big shots on board, it's difficult to find information on building and renovating which tells you about the stuff that can and frequently does go wrong – the things you don't find out until the wet work is finished and it's too late.

'I am the expert and I know what I am doing,' is the mantra of a project manager I met at the Seattle Coffee shop in Constantia which, during the renovations, became my refuge. Sipping my extra dry, short, skinny cappuccino and bashing at my laptop, people would invariably comment on the building series, which, as my editor Jacqui L'Ange put it, became something of a weekly newspaper blog. I listened very carefully to what they had to say and took their advice seriously: like new parents doling out colic tips and moral support, renovators love sharing, and some of the best tips are from fellow shoppers whom you meet in the queue while you are having your paw-paws weighed. This is the opposite attitude to that of the aforementioned self-appointed-expert project manager – not the type of person I'd like to work with on a building project.

Everyone is an expert in his or her field, and there is the rub. No matter how fancy you may be, you may not have a handle on the broader picture. An electrician friend quips, 'I know my sockets but I have no clue when it comes to UGs (plumbing underground pipes).' A developer of a retirement village, working with the best in the field, admits that he erred when installing stylish taps and door handles; pity that the elderly residents require contortionist skills to operate them.

With South Africa's booming building industry, everyone is a builder and barriers to the industry are often nil. Do a quickie bricklayer course and you can consider yourself one of the *baksteen mense* (bricklayers). In theory, it means that we can all become builders – and why not?

One of the aims of the series, and this book, has been to demystify the building process. As long as your house is under 500 square metres, you don't need to be an architect to draw up plans. You *do* need to know the format, scale requirements and how to colour code the whole shebang. Granted, most of us may not have what it takes to draw up our own plans. However, there is a lot that we can get involved with during the building process. It is your building. Do not be afraid.

Of course, we need pointers to steer us in the right direction. Even mega-budget developments can result in poor choices – check out the toilets at your neighbourhood mall for disaster zones of note; there is no room for a trolley, let alone for a pram or wheelchair. Taps on hideous basins send water spurting in every direction – except your hands. Even with all that money in the kitty, 'experts' often get it wrong.

Bottom line is, whoever we are – homeowners with just enough to do a quickie facelift of the kitchen or developers with lots of *latkes* – we need to do our best to bring our building project in on time, on budget, and looking great.

Talking of surprises, a publicist called me the other day while I was in the editing stages of this book. Her brother, who lives in New York, is renovating his Brownstone and wants to know if he can order a copy through Amazon. As the title of the series stated, my articles chronicled the story of my house. It's a house in Cape Town, which has earned the moniker 'Slaapstadt' (sleepy town) for good reason. What lessons could a building book inspired by the vicissitudes of renovating in the Mother City possibly have for the Big Apple? 'Building is building, wherever you are,' the publicist replied. 'Besides, the jokes will do him good.'

This book is not an A-Z of building. It's about one family's experience of building in the Cape: a mom (that's me); a dad (Greg – aka Greg the Builder, who isn't a builder by training or trade – and you will soon see why we call him that); and their two gorgeous daughters (Jessie and Sarah). Please enjoy the ride because the joys far outweigh the stresses – and there's nothing quite like the smell of fresh paint in the morning.

PROLOGUE:

Before we **begin...**

Ladies and gentlemen, before you begin your building project, allow me to ask you a question: Is it absolutely necessary to overhaul your life with building works? Can you simply, by rearranging the goal posts, find the means to a different end? Everything is relative, as may be seen from the following parable, which is a staple in many anthologies of Jewish humour.

A poor man went to his Rabbi and cried 'Rabbi, help me, my house is too small. My wife, my children, my in-laws – it's too much. I can't take it anymore.' Sagely, the Rabbi replied, 'My son, take your cow and put it in your lounge.' The man gesticulated in a way that suggested he thought the Rabbi quite mad, but did what he was told. He returned the next day and pleaded, 'Rabbi, it is much worse.' The Rabbi said, 'Now I want you take your hens, your horse, your plow, and your geese into the house.' And so it continued, with the man having to bring all his possessions into the house. Finally, when the house was so crowded that there was barely room to get a foot in the door, the Rabbi told the man, 'Right. Now, I want you to take the animals and your tools out of the house.' A few days later the man bumped into the Rabbi again. 'Wow, it's a miracle,' said the man. 'The house is wonderful. I never realised how large the space is.'

For contemporary resonance, visualise your horrible bedroom: bring in the jumbo plasma TV, children's desks, dog, cat. Move in mother-in-law; entice wife from spare room. After a few days, take everything out. Whatalotofspace-yougot. Breathe, reassess. Still want to renovate? Perhaps you can turf out some possessions and achieve the same effect?

If you are still determined to carry on, I recommend the 'G & T equalizer'.

Building being building, things can go wrong. We don't for one minute advocate substance dependence to get you through, but gin and tonic was our on-site beverage. It has an undeniable colonial resonance, conjuring up languid relaxation in an exotic location. It is not a drink that can be slugged on the run. You need the tonic water, a slice of lemon, ice, a decent glass. And when you are standing in mud on a building site, it feels like nectar from the gods.

WEZA

SECTION ONE

planning

Chapter 1:

Getting started – **locating your hot spots**

From the moment we glimpsed our house, we felt a good karma. It spoke to us. Sometimes it spoke to us too loudly. Design-wise, it had its faults. Haphazard additions meant that the communal living spaces were cramped and punctuated by unnecessary archways and walls. There was no garage access directly into the house.

One of its key features, which literally took our breath away, was a glass conservatory, which, we think, was meant to be the dining room. It looked like something out of a décor magazine: spectacular angular glass panes, buttressed with galvanised steel, topped off with a sloping roof. The people who built the house were in the glass business and we were told that the glass was also bullet proof, which was good to know.

So much for first impressions. The room was freezing in winter, boiling in summer. (One summer's day I put some eggs on the table and they practically fried from the heat.) When we sat at the table at night, we were mirrored in the highly reflective roof. Most unnerving. It was the kind of effect that one might expect to find in an exotic Las Vegas hotel – not that I have ever stayed in one of those. Dimension wise, the room was a tight squeeze. Once you were seated at one end, you were locked in for the evening. We soon moved the dining-room table into the entrance hall and the glass room became a dumping ground for the children's paraphernalia and the exercise bike that no one ever uses.

The glass cracked. When it rained, we had to arrange buckets to catch the water. This horrible room was a renovation priority – and an important design lesson for us: superb aesthetics mean nothing if there is zero functionality. Our glasshouse may have been a success in another context – a shady forest setting, for example. It may have suited another family who enjoy sun baking in their own home. It did not work for us.

Our homes are all about function. We need spaces that not only contain us but also nurture – rather than alienate – us. The traffic in your home is important. If your children's career aspirations include being the next Spice Girls or Freshlyground, perhaps you need to consider building a soundproof studio and ditching the playroom. As homeowners we have to design what suits our families and not what suits a décor magazine. Above all, we have to accomplish this amazing transformation within budgetary constraints. In this regard, there is a lovely maxim doing the rounds at the moment about credit cards: remember that the maximum you can spend is a limit, not a target.

At first, our dreams about changing the house were purely academic. As it turns out, that was for the best. By the time we got our demolition men on site, we knew exactly what we wanted. People have said, 'You were sensible to have waited.' Really, we can't take credit; we would have loved an instant gratification scenario – like being whizzed away to a Disney World-type resort as they do in extreme makeover shows on telly, to return a week later to a brand-new house. The truth is, for the first five years we were merely tenants in our house. The owners were living abroad and still deciding whether or not to return. Luckily, for us, they decided to sell just before the property boom. Initially, we reasoned that we would be overcapitalising if we renovated. The children were babies and who could face the disruption?

Some people have funds to keep renovating. We wanted to do it, and do it once. Still, the time was never right. We remembered what one wise auntie said to us many moons ago, when we were pondering if it was time to start a family. 'There is never a right time. Babies bring their own luck,' adding for good measure, *'Tsum glik, tsum shlimazel.'* (For better, for worse.) She was right. Building is about growth and we liked all the metaphors inherent in that.

Property values soared and halted our dithering. Our pretty suburb with leafy outlook and mountain views became hot property. Then the house across the road came up for rent. If ever there was a sign from a higher power that the time was finally nigh, this was it. Who could argue with this logic? We had saved the money. There were no more excuses.

The word 'renovation' tends to sound less scary than the word 'building'. Scrap the euphemisms: it's building. There's digging and mud and mess and the poor garden you worked so hard at landscaping will be mucked up.

Some people camp out in one room and use the bath as a sink. Not us. We knew that we wanted to alter every room, except one. Although there was a matter of rental to pay, building goes a lot faster if you are off site.

During a few frenzied weeks of drawing up our plans, we looked at other people's renovations – and what I call the '*phadrush* factor'. *Phadrush* is a lovely Yiddish word which, loosely translated, means 'regret', but is tinged with self-deprecating humour. We know many people who have done lovely renovations but not got what they needed. After living in the house for eight years, we knew what we needed.

Getting what you need (which does not always equate with what you want, or how to achieve champagne tastes with beer money)

So, what did we need? To answer that, let me quote the words of Jona Lewie's catchy 80s synthpop hit 'You'll Always Find Me in the Kitchen at Parties'. Party or no party, you will always find us in our kitchen. It is the heart of our home and pumping. One afternoon, while the family was mulling over our renovation plans and munching flapjacks, there was a moment of pure epiphany: Jessie and Sarah never do their school work in their bedrooms. Invariably, they gather around the small bench top in the kitchen and do their work while I am cooking. They follow me into my office and sit on the floor while I hack away on the computer. Greg comes in and discusses his day. Besides the bathroom, my office is the smallest room in our little nest. Talk about Crowded House.

Decompressing bedrooms

Experts from the stress busting website (www.stressbusting.co.uk) suggest that in order to de-stress bedrooms for children, we should remove all distractions such as computers, TVs, and computer games. By purging the room of flickering machines and turning the heat down (as in heaters), we can help our children to relax and ultimately sleep better, improve concentration, score higher marks in exams, and be less hormonally hyper. Makes a lot of sense. Us parents need to apply the same principles and decompress our conjugal domiciles.

I conducted an informal survey among friends and colleagues: for the most part, children's desks have become white elephants. Children tend to gravitate to the kitchen, dining room, living room – or their parents' room. Leisure time is spent anywhere there is a TV or computer. Thanks to wireless Internet and laptop access kids can, and do, work anywhere. Teenagers need to assert their tribal identity and this entails only being part of the family when it suits them (and probably won't involve your designs for living).

The plan came to us in a flash: we would build an office upstairs for me, and put the children's desks on another side of the room. The novels, art books and stationery in my office would find a new home. (*Oygotinka*, you should have seen what came out of that tiny office, when we moved out – don't even go there!) By building an office/library upstairs, we would free up a room downstairs. This would become Greg's office. His old office would become much-needed lounge space (no more cabin fever) and the entrance hall would become another bedroom, allowing Jessie and Sarah to have their own rooms.

Technology was an important consideration, with the setting up of a wireless internet high on the priority list. The open layout of the living section would allow us to configure our house as a wireless hot spot so that we could work with a minimum of cables, share data, and use one printer. Plus, our children were desperate to get onto instant messaging and into the 'dingi' (*see Where should I place my router?*) that get their generation revved up.

The *Amazing Race* was about to begin. For those of you who don't watch television, the *Amazing Race* is a reality show where contestants, in paired teams, race around the world in pursuit of the million-dollar prize. Each episode is marked by roadblocks and detours which test contestants' nerves to the hilt. It is a combination of skill, physical endurance, foresight, planning, optimism and luck. Sounds exactly like building.

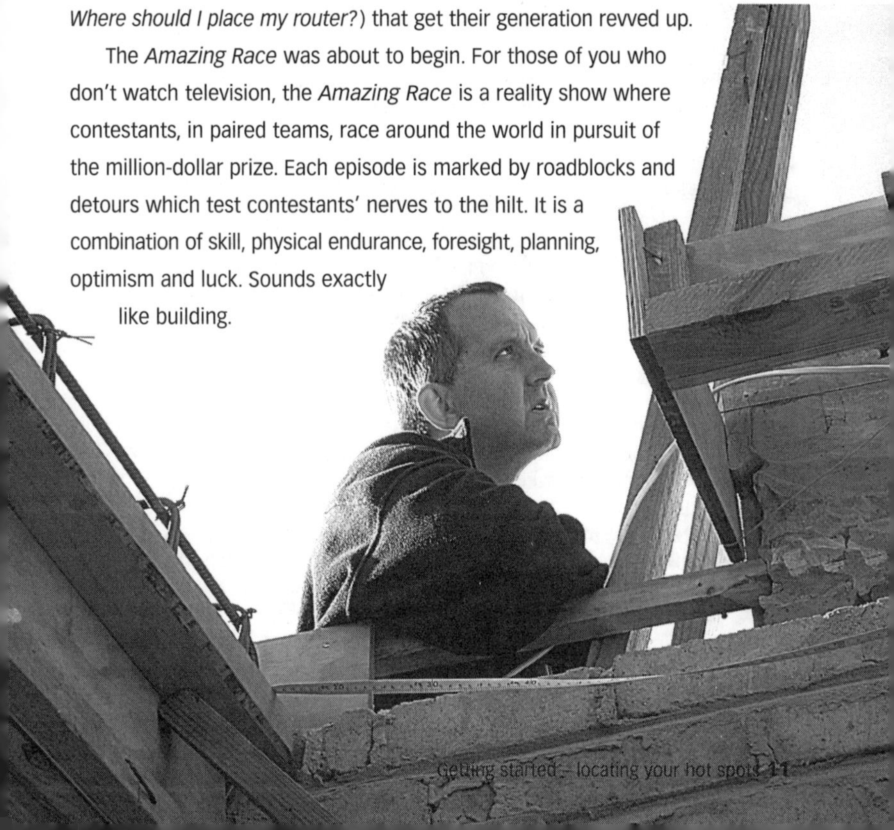

Jokes aside, we invoked the *Amazing Race* as a morale booster for the family when we hit the inevitable stumbling blocks. In doing so, we conjured up an escapist device to step away from the building and see it as just that – building. 'Right Jessie and Sarah, your task for today is to stay out of the way of painter no 1 and painter no 2 who had a barney Friday night at a party.' We wished this was TV. A million bucks reward would have been a nice injection into the bank account, to counter the draining of our savings.

We began the Amazing Race to get our house on the road in a seemingly impossible 15 weeks – before builders' holiday on 16 December. We started on 1 September – 104 years to the day that construction began on the New York Stock Exchange. Bet you didn't know that. Then again, neither did we. Everyone said we were deluded, absolutely *mal* and *meshugah*. We would never finish in that time. No way.

Were they right? Greg the Builder said that if the BMW Pavilion at Cape Town's V&A Waterfront could be completed in 33 weeks, then he could wrap it up in 15, with co-operation of course from the South Atlantic high-pressure zone. Translated: it better not rain until the roof was up.

Where should I place my router?

In the past, whenever we wanted to do something vaguely technological, we were told that our systems were not compatible and that we needed an upgrade to power the dingus. A 'dingus' is what our IT friends Daniel and Gary call anything technologically related. It could be the hardware (i.e. the wireless router hub you need to set up a hot spot) or a manoeuvre or trick. The word is accompanied by lots of sign language and gesticulations.

An electrician won't necessarily give you the correct advice on where to place the bells and whistles for the many dingi (plural of dingus) you'll need – be it a home entertainment centre with a floating plasma TV screen, or how best to position the base station for your wireless hub so that the signal can feed into the areas you need it most. There's no point having an upstairs office if the signal is blocked by the concrete slab. The same principle holds for sound systems that are beamed to multiple rooms. Position is everything: ask a computer technician for advice.

Although techno emporiums are well stocked, their personnel often have absolutely no knowledge of the workings of the dingus you are about to buy and whether it suits your floor plan. We found a guardian angel at Computer Mania in Cavendish Square. It is worth buying a mouse that you don't need in order to get advice from Dr Andrew, as he is called by many, with good reason. CM are not national but they have a list of dingi on their website (www.computermania.co.za). Note that the person who installs the dingus for the TV, DVD, satellite, etc., is not the same person who installs the dingus for the computer.

Chapter 2:

Design – from broad stroke to nitty-gritty

Designing is a constant negotiation – between partners, and between what you want and what you can afford.

When designing your living-space specs, always take cognisance of the lifestyle dynamics of your household. It is also prudent to consider the ramifications of your ideas for re-sale purposes. Poorly considered renovations costing huge amounts may add zero value to your house. One house, which has been for sale in our area for ages, has ultra expensive finishes and a chef's kitchen. One little problem: it is quite simply in the wrong location. It needs to be set amidst a couple of hectares in Bishopscourt, Lower Houghton or St Lucia. Instead, it occupies a corner plot and overlooks a link road between the highway and the main road. As of writing, it is still vacant and the owners have decamped for sunnier vistas in Mauritius.

Unlike a new building, where you can start from scratch, with renovating you are obviously constrained by what is already there – unless you are prepared to raze the lot to the ground, in which case you aren't renovating at all.

Consider very carefully the traffic that flows through your house. If you have young children, a floating cantilevered glass staircase is probably not a good idea. If you are a senior citizen with hip and shoulder replacements, a helter-skelter staircase is definitely not a good idea.

Some time ago, I came across an article in an American publication that profiled architects, designers and decorators. Each of them was photographed in their living space, which was juxtaposed with their design ethos. They all espoused a minimalist aesthetic in their work. Meanwhile, their own homes were the antithesis of sleek: crammed with furniture, books and objects. One conceded the contradiction but qualified his home style, saying that the bulk of his work centred on industrial architecture and the needs are different in this domain. Exactly.

During the design phase, our architectural draughtsperson was brilliant in that he drew up what we wanted and did not impose his own vision. He did however make suggestions as to how we could make the spaces work – within a budget and within the limits of what was structurally possible and would not cause grief to our local council.

Our house

Our house was afflicted with what I call the 'iced-cake effect'. Think of birthday cakes assembled from chunks; the icing conceals some of it, but you can still see the joins. This is the inevitable result of renovating in spurts – you do one room a year because you don't have the finances to complete in one go. If this is how you must proceed, try to conceptualise the entire design before you begin, and complete it section by section according to your plans.

Our house went all higgledy-piggledy. We wanted to bring everything into line, unifying the entire structure. And we felt that it was best to design within the parameters of the house footprint.

When renovating, always remember that your designs are not cast in steel. I invoke the S-word, because when we decided to build a first floor area, I jumped up and down at the prospect of a balcony with a modernist fancy-shmancy steel railing. Then reality hit: steel is not ideal for this particular balcony, which is visible from the street.

Number one was the issue of privacy: see-through rails would mean always having to sit nicely, legs crossed, no vpl's (visible panty lines) in sight. Number two: the balcony situated on the east side is likely to be thrashed by the south-easter. Open railings do not provide wind protection. Number three: open railings are not the safest for children who like to dangle their limbs through the spaces and cause grief to their parents. And last, but not least, the bill: at least 15 grand for steel.

The solution: we built a brick wall, which encloses the space, provides privacy, wind protection and a measure of safety. Architecturally, the box structure echoes the cube shape of the extension and balances it visually. It is now a feature, rather than an appendage; an elevated version of a tree-house, a space to chill out in. It was initially difficult for me to concede that Greg was right – a flimsy steel railing would have looked ridiculous.

I wanted double-volume doors, but this would have blown the budget for the kitchen. And we decided to retain the wooden window frames because we feel that this suits the character of the house. (It all adds up: if you replace all your windows with aluminium, you are facing a hefty bill – not only must you purchase additional windows, but you need to replace the old ones.)

Design does not stop at the planning stage – be prepared to design-as-you-build. What looks good on paper does not always look great when the building dagga (not the type you smoke) is smeared onto those bricks. Of course you are limited in the number of changes you can make (otherwise you have to go through the schlep of re-submitting to council). But there is a great deal that one can do during the wet work and finishing phases. By finishing, we don't mean decorating, which is another story altogether.

Speak your mind

If there is one thing I have learnt from this process: you need to keep your focus during the building process, and if something does not look good, you need to say so. It goes further than that. It is no good simply asking, 'How straight is that wall?' The question is: how does that wall function? Does it do what we need it to?

Non-load-bearing walls may be tweaked and moved. A few centimetres can make all the difference. Before building the internal walls, we played around with the placement of a diagonal wall that screens the entrance from the kitchen, by moving sheets of wood around and physically interacting in the space to monitor the flow. The wall is still placed according to plan, yet tweaked just enough to make it work perfectly.

We did the same outside a new toilet in my upstairs area. Nevertheless, after the wall went up, we could see that it wasn't right. It was an internal wall, so we bashed it down and moved it 200 mm to the left. It worked. During plastering, we asked our team to add a little more plastering dagga here, a little less there. It made all the difference.

With all the building work, the floors got pretty messed up and we were forced to re-tile. With its terracotta-like tiles, our house conjured up an image of African red mud floors, which couldn't be more different than the current trend towards beige marshmallow stone floors. Ferreting out a terracotta-look ceramic tile turned out to be quite a feat, but we did eventually find what we want. (*See Tip box: Floored*)

If you spot something that isn't right, now is the time to speak up. There's a narrow window of opportunity when things may be rectified. Remember that builders and architects and designers are not perfect. Mistakes happen. It may well be your error, not theirs. Don't have *phadrus* later when you bitch to your spouse that you thought something was wrong. He or she will rightly ask, 'So why didn't you say something at the time?'

Things to consider when designing

This is not an all-inclusive list but it's a start. Experts start regaling you with talk of a 'gourmet kitchen', 'double-volume interiors', 'designer this and designer that'. It is very seductive language, but at the end of the project, you may find that you have lost sight of the bigger picture. When designing, consider the following:

Orientation: Are the main bedrooms of your house and living areas on the northern side of the house? If so, you live in what is generally referred to as a north-facing house. Consider the sunrise and sunset in your area. The closer you are to the eastern side of a mountain or *koppie*, the earlier your sunset will be. (It is not the official sunset time but you'll be in the shade.) Conversely, the closer you are to the western side of a mountain or any other large structure, the later the sun will shine on your house in the morning.

Flow to outdoor areas: If entertaining is important to you, then the access points from your living area – including kitchen – to outdoor braai and swimming areas must be considered. You don't want to traipse through the lounge carrying a marinated fish all the way to the braai area. A door to the patio will save you mess and kids walking through with water from the pool liberally pouring over the floors.

Outside floor finishes: Brick-paved areas in direct sunlight may generate heat. If they are in fully shaded areas, they may stay cold and wet and grow moss. Could be slippery when wet.

Storage: Lawnmower, garden tools, brooms, vacuum cleaners – where will they live? Think about a home for the stuff that clutters our lives. If you need it, find a place for it. If not, ditch it. Sheds or wendy houses are good options, but you may need plans, depending on size and whether electricity or water is involved.

Granny flats: Good for re-sale and a godsend as a pad for the teenager-who-wants-to-be-alone. For privacy, include own access, and a toilet and shower.

Direct access from garage: This is a big plus from a security point of view, when it comes to re-selling a home. But people often forget about it – or they place the garage with direct access into the main bedroom!

Access panels and DBs (distribution boards): They may not be aesthetically beautiful, but you want them to be accessible – especially when the lights go out. Place them in a hidden spot that is easy to get to.

Bathrooms and toilets: Do you need a guest loo or a family toilet? Can you have both? It may be possible to redirect piping and create additional toilets without too much extra cost.

Kitchen planning: If you hate cooking and eat out all the time, what is the point of having a 'gourmet kitchen' when a 'take-out kitchen' with microwave will do? Use the extra space for a wine cellar. However, do remember that kitchens are important for re-sale. Downsize if you will, but keep the basics intact.

Traffic flows: How busy is your household? Have children who like to skateboard round the house? Put in a suitable floor. If you have anyone with a disability, you may want to put in handrails and soft coverings on walls to prevent injury.

Security: Unless you live in a gated community with 24-hr surveillance, or in a utopia where security is not an issue, you cannot duck this one. Security needs to be considered early on and fine-tuned as you build. When designing our staircase, I merrily insisted on having a window at step number three, until our draughtsperson correctly pointed out that this would make an easy entry point.

Absolute no-no's:

• Windows over baths • Stoves next to fridges • Toilets off the kitchen
• Floor-level windows in areas subject to flooding • Long narrow passages

Hot and cold flushes

Insulation goes hand in hand with heating and cooling design. Good insulating materials in the roof will save you in the long term, and are available in a wide range. They are well worth installing, especially as the cost of heating and cooling increases. If you have built up, then the slab usually creates a warmer space downstairs, and the upstairs area will be the one that will need insulation. If you want to install ducted air-conditioning systems (sometimes called split systems), then you must consult your electrician as these units can use massive amounts of electricity. You may even need three-phase power. The same issues apply for fancy powerful heating systems.

Solar heating roof panels are a further long-term cost-saving system, especially if you have a north-facing aspect to the roof that you can use. Sustainable energy-saving systems should be compulsory in this country, but let's not get into politics.

Floored

Terracotta is earthy. It grounds us. We like it. The colour does not show up dirt. It makes the interiors feel warm, and it's cool to walk on barefoot in summer. But it is not in vogue. **TIP: Do not be intimidated by sales talk or friends who try and persuade you to follow the latest trend.** In the interest of keeping up with trends, we bought stone tiles on appro just to see what they looked like. Next to the whitish paint we had chosen, they looked grubby and dirty. Wood was tempting, but the hardwood ranges were way out of our budget, and didn't pass a scratch test (when I dragged a chair across a sample, it left ridges). I do not want to be terrified that my beautiful wooden floors are being wrecked by children on scooters. Wood is not recommended for houses with dogs with long nails. The terracotta ceramic tile won.

Avoid that gutted feeling

Try to avoid box gutters, unless essential. A box gutter is a gutter created where a roof comes down to the normal ceiling/gutter level, only to be met by either another roof or wall. In other words, if you rolled a tennis ball off that roof, it would not fall to the ground – it would end up in the gutter, or jammed against the wall. Box gutters sometimes run right over your living areas, so you need to make certain they really are correctly designed and built.

Builders sometimes battle with box gutters because it is not always easy to create the necessary 'fall' of the gutter – in other words the slight pitch at which gutters fall, so that water flows out. (Architects/designers of course don't have to worry about that sort of practical problem – that's for the builder to sort out!)

If a box gutter is unavoidable, get up on the roof yourself and make quite certain that you are happy with the design and engineering of the gutter. There are different ways to build them, using various materials such as shutterply timber covered with heavy-duty waterproofing membrane, or aluminium moulded to the correct shape. But remember, they have to be 100% waterproof, even in a heavy downpour. You must make sure that even if the gutter were to overflow, there are safety catchment areas either side – otherwise you'll have water coming in through your ceiling some dark and stormy night, when you really don't need it.

Box gutters must be cleaned regularly. A nifty new invention called the gutter-brush may be worth installing. It's like a brush placed upside down in the gutter, with the bristles sticking up; the theory is that leaves and debris get stuck in the bristles, even swept away by wind, allowing only water into the gutter itself.

Chapter 3:

Mother knows best – **the ins and outs of planning**

Consider the following story told to me by my mother, which she heard from a friend from bridge (as in the card game). The bridge friend's daughter recently renovated her house. The daughter engaged 'the best architect in all Johannesburg'. The mother asked her daughter, 'But darling aren't you taking too many walls away? Won't your house fall down? It doesn't look right.' The daughter chided: 'Ma, this is really a subject that you know nothing about. We have the top architect, the best engineer, and a master builder. They know what they are doing.' Maybe, but they got it wrong on this occasion. When the props were removed, the house almost fell down. At huge expense, engineers had to be brought in to construct special steel girders. The moral: listen to your mother. If you don't have a mum, phone a friend and ask to borrow his or hers.

Things my momma taught me (1): Patience is a virtue

This was brought home (if you'll excuse the pun) when we were in the process of getting our plans through Council. Our draughtsman is a lovely man. He managed to keep the peace between my husband and myself when we were thrashing out what we envisaged our home could become. He drew what we wanted – or both agreed on. He had adhered to Council specifications in drawing up our plans and assured us that the plans would eventually go through.

If your draughtsperson/architect says, 'Leave it to me, I'll follow up,' it is certainly your prerogative to let them continue walking your plans. You're paying them, why should you stand in the queue? If time is on your side, go for it. However, we did not have time on our hands.

The plans went in. One of the inspectors was ill and the Council was short staffed. Be patient, advised our man. I had been told not to call for a progress report before four weeks had elapsed after submission. Four weeks went by and then six and we got anxious.

Having plans passed is a bit like natural childbirth without an epidural (been there and done that – afterwards you forget the pain and insist that it wasn't that bad). We were sweating bullets. Rent was being paid on the house across the road, and still our plans had not moved through Zoning.

With the clock ticking, one fine Monday I called our local Council and requested an update on our plans. (You don't need to be an expert to do this. You simply need your reference/erf number and off you go. The City of Johannesburg – see contact list on page 96 – allows homeowners to do an online search to track plans. Such clever people.)

The very polite official said that I could call on Friday as he still had a way to go before he got to our number. I hung up. Something niggled. What happens if our plans are incomplete? Are we then likely to be shunted to the back of the queue? Will we have to wait another week before our number comes up again?

I called the nice official, no doubt interrupting him from his work yet again. Did he have everything he needed? He checked our file. Actually, no he did not. The engineer's report had not been included. As the registered homeowner I had not signed a certain blue form and measurements were missing from one of the elevations. The Council office was closing in twenty minutes but if I raced there, I could sign the form. I did this and he kindly wrote in the measurements, which I signed.

And so the plans were able to move out of his department. Apparently, plans are often sent in incomplete, or with incorrect dimensions. I discovered this in the following two weeks when I made several trips to the Council as the plans moved from department to department. I interacted with many homeowners who were walking their plans through.

Too many people blame councils for dragging their feet, but having been there and watched what goes on, I think we can all endeavour to do our bit and make sure that our plans are ship-shape. That would save the Council wasted effort scrutinising plans and sending them back for amendments, often for things that the draughtspeople should really get right the first time. One day, I saw a gentleman provided with coloured pencils because his architect had not coloured in his plans. That is customer service.

Submitting Plans

You will need Council approval for any additions to your property not shown on the original plan. (Sometimes plans are approved for an alteration or addition but don't get built. If you have approved plans, but the work has never been done, you shouldn't have to go through the *megillah* (process) again, especially if the plans are fairly recent.) You may need engineering plans if you are going up, or intend to build on steep slopes. You'll also need approval for anything outside, like a swimming pool, Jacuzzi, or spa, because these structures involve excavation of the land, electricity supply, plumbing and drainage. Council approval is required for any boundary walls.

Remember, as long as your house is less than 500 square metres, you do not have to be an architect or draughtsperson to draw up plans. Requirements may differ from region to region, so it's best to check with the relevant authority before submitting your plans. Your Council can advise what is necessary for your type of dwelling.

Broadly speaking, you have to submit a site plan, layout and drainage installation drawings, and engineering reports, if you are adding additional storeys, lighting and so on. A fire protection plan is necessary if the building will be used by the public. Plans must be colour coded: proposed buildings (red), existing buildings, structures and pools on the site (uncoloured), and buildings to be demolished in dotted lines.

The application documents and plans must show the name of the person who prepared them. An architect, land surveyor or professional engineer must show his or her registration number. Additional information (e.g. coverage and floor area calculations, reinforced concrete details) may be required. No tippex, stickers or omissions are permitted on any plans, so it is imperative to check that everything is correct when submitting.

Council requirements change from time to time, so it is best to call them one more time and check. Submit your plans to the municipality where you pay rates. (See contact details at the back of the book for plan submission in our major cities.)

Things my momma taught me (2): Where to draw the line

On that note, building lines and regulations need to be carefully checked. The boundary line is the edge of the property – where your property ends and the neighbour's begins. In most cases, you have one, two, three and sometimes even four neighbours (if you are in a panhandle). Usually you have some Council property, such as roads or part of your driveway, on one or more sides.

The building line is usually, but not always, set back away from the boundary line by a distance varying from 0 to 4.5 metres and sometimes even further. The exception is garages, which can in most cases be built on the boundary line. How close you can build to your boundary line is also known as the 'set-back'. If you take them your property plans, Council will tell you what the set-back is, depending on whether you are building on the ground floor, extending upwards, or both.

In some cases, Council will permit you to build over the normal set-back, that is, closer to the boundary line than is usually allowed. This permission is also known as a departure. When you are preparing your plans you have to give careful thought to your neighbours' privacy, the possibility of obstructing their views, or any other aspects of your proposed building which Council might consider objectionable. (For example, they will usually object to you building two-storey structures with windows that allow you to leer into your neighbour's bedroom.)

There are also usually height restrictions when building. In most cases, the set-back from your neighbours varies between one and three metres on the ground floor. The set-back from Council property is usually 4.5 metres. If you are going to build up, that set-back may have to be increased, or will be allowed only with your neighbour's written consent.

Big tip: Be very careful of giving written consent to your neighbour's plans to extend their house when you are tired and frazzled and when they try and put you under pressure. You may bitterly regret having tried to be a nice neighbour. A double storey with a pitched roof, one metre away from the boundary wall, will be very big and ugly and blot out a lot of the sun. Your signature on someone else's plans could devalue your property in an instant. Trying to reverse the process, especially after your neighbour has begun to build, may lead to a legal nightmare.

Then there is the Bulk Factor (BF). In simple terms, this is the percentage of the building on the size of the erf. The BF allowed in most residential areas is fifty percent. In other words, if you have a 500 square metre erf, you will be allowed to build a 250 square metre home. BF may vary from suburb to suburb, and Council may allow departures from these restrictions as well.

And the walls, came tumbling down ....

Which walls can you knock out without Council approval? There are three kinds of brick walls in most houses. These are: 115 mm (as thick as one brick), 230 mm (as thick as two bricks) and 280 mm (two bricks thick with 50 mm cavity in between) – also known as a cavity wall. These are usually the exteriors walls to your house to allow ventilation. The double and cavity walls are your load-bearing walls. They are holding up the roof or slab above it.

As a general rule, you don't need permission for internal renovation work, provided you are not knocking out load-bearing (structural support) walls. Internal renovations, like re-doing your bathroom and toilet, do not require council approval. You are free to rip out your tiles, toilets, baths and showers, put in new vanities, change the position of your toilets and showers without Council's permission. You can rip out internal/single walls and re-tile your roof without approval. You cannot, however, build a fireplace without approval as there are fire regulations involved. If you live in a block of flats or a townhouse complex, almost all of the above will be subject to the strata or body corporate (BC) rules.

We were delighted with the friendliness and helpfulness of our local building inspectors (South Peninsula Municipality) – they offered outstanding service and gave invaluable assistance and advice. A word of warning: Inspectors do the rounds and will see very quickly when building is occurring. They can fine you if you build without permission. The golden rule is to be safe rather than sorry; check any changes to your property with your local council and building inspector. While you're at it, make sure you get insurance cover for your site, builders, etc. Check with your broker that you are fully covered in case anyone falls off a ladder.

The Great Gatsby Mother

During one of my many trips to the Council offices, I encountered an irate homeowner who had erected a garden shed sans plans. She said that her sister, drawing on her own shed-building experience, had assured her that she didn't require permission from Council. Sista was wrong. Irate Homeowner hung her head in shame. She admitted that her mother had warned her that she was making a mistake.

This takes us back to the importance of heeding mother's advice. To rephrase an old joke: What's the difference between the responses of a Jewish mother and Italian mother to their daughter's renovation woes? Italian mother: If you don't get this builder off the site, I'll kill him! Jewish mother: If you don't get rid of this builder, I'll kill myself! Guilt, smieldt. Whatever works.

My foolproof building formula: If you don't want to mess up when renovating, make sure you have a mother in the wings – otherwise, it will not work out. She doesn't have to be Jewish but it helps. She doesn't have to be a Johannesburg mother, but it helps. I've been told that New York mothers are also pretty good. It is all in the *kvetching* (nagging) antennae, which need to be primed to avert disasters.

Although I have lived in Cape Town for more than a decade and it pains me to let the region down, I have to confess that it is best if the mother is a Johannesburg mother because Joburg mothers don't give up. Cape Town mothers have their hearts in the right place. They mean well, but they lose their focus when it is a beautiful day. Given the vagaries of weather and the Cape Doctor thrashing about, that's understandable. Who wants to nag, if you can go to the beach and eat a Gatsby with smoked salmon and cream cheese?

A Gatsby, for the uninitiated, is a Cape Town culinary delight – a baguette crammed with a multitude of ingredients and *slap* (greasy) chips. The online Food Network (www.foodnetwork.com/food) describes it as a 'French loaf stuffed with hot chips, French polony, and a salad dressing'. They say that the Gatsby is to Cape Town what the hot dog is to New York.

Gatsbys proved to be the way to our *baksteen mense*'s (bricklayers') hearts. When our builders were having a bad concrete day, we knew that a Gatsby from Osmans, the fish shop down the road, was a sure way to get them into the swing of things. Fish Gatsbys, calamari Gatsbys, samp and beans Gatsbys, pap en wors Gatsbys – Osmans have every variation of Gatsby with their signature special spice.

My correspondents in Durban tell me that Bunny Chow is the way to builders' hearts in the curry city. The Bunny Chow is similar to the Gatsby, but not as stylish. Bunny Chows are made from quarters, halves or full loaves of bread, which are gutted and crammed with curry, veggies and whatever else is going. Best if the bread is on the stale side – too fresh, and the bottom falls out. (I know I am culturally biased, but I think Gatsbys have an advantage over

Bunnies as they can be shared. You can cut a Gatsby in half with a very sharp knife but if you cut a Bunny … *gemors*.)

If Cape Town has the Gatsby and Durban the Bunny, what does the trick in Gauteng? Whatever the menu, you need a mother on site because she knows when it is time to go and buy lunch.

The plans were not even through Zoning, and Hessie (my mother) was already asking if I had taken care of the food for the builders. I told her I was not a catering committee. She was not fazed. 'Wait. You'll see.' Sure enough, it came to pass: one sweltering day, even the flies were vrekking, and the men were not hard at work. I offered lunch. Hallelujah. They were revived. I kept the news from my mother. (I was embarrassed, what can I say?) She found out from Jessie and Sarah, who broke the family code of silence. 'Did I tell you or what? *Shemzach* (shame on you) for not giving them lunch for the first two weeks. No wonder progress has been slow.' Hessie came to stay with us mid-way through the renovations, and I simply handed over the food portfolio to her.

Jokes aside, food is critical to the success of the renovating project. Building is exhausting, kilojoule-burning work. An agony aunt once quipped that her Granny had wisely said that the best way to avoid conflict in a marriage is to take one's clothes off when fighting. The same goes for building: the best way to avoid conflict on site is to keep your builders, and yourselves, well fed.

DO I NEED COUNCIL APPROVAL FOR …

YES

- Renovations which alter the footprint or height depicted on the original approved plans
- Internal renovations which involve load-bearing walls
- If you require a departure (neighbour's privacy, boundary or set-back, second dwelling/granny flat)
- If you wish to exceed the BF (bulk factor)
- A new fireplace
- A new or changed gas installation
- Swimming pools, Jacuzzis or spas
- Boundary walls
- Wendy houses/garden sheds over a certain size, depending on where you live

NO (OR MAYBE – RULES DO CHANGE, SO CHECK!)

- Some boundary walls and fences
- Revamps of existing bathroom (with no structural changes)
- Roof re-tiling, with no structural changes, and using same materials (so check before switching from a tin roof to thatch)
- Internal renovations that involve only non-load-bearing walls

Chapter 4:

Choosing a builder – the dartboard approach

A few years ago, a selection of JSE listed companies chosen by a young child was by far the best performer out of a group of 'dummy' stock portfolios set up by some of the country's top financial advisers.

How did he manage it? The youngster selected the portfolio using the dartboard approach – he threw darts at a page of listed company names. Where the dart hit, that company's shares were bought. This completely random and unscientific approach worked – that time.

In my experience, and judging from others whom we have met down renovation lane, it may well be argued that the dartboard method is a perfectly good way to choose a builder. We know people who have had problems with accredited builders and others who had problems with unaccredited contractors. Almost everyone we know can relate at least one bad building experience – the builder did not finish the job, the builder made off with the money, the walls were skew, the roof leaked, and they never finished the floors.

The building industry is on a roll. The bullish property market is driving the renovation boom, and good contractors appear to have more work than they can handle.

Homeowners need to be alert at all times and keep the following in mind: no matter whom you choose, things are unlikely to go without hiccups. Brace yourself for the ride.

So how do you choose your builders and how do you find good sub-contractors?

One option is to go to the NHBRC (National Home Builders Registration Council) (see contacts list on page 97) and ask them for a list of builders in your area.

Look up Builders in the Yellow Pages. In the Cape Town directory, there are nearly seven pages of builders listed. Hopefully a builder or company that can afford to advertise in the Yellow Pages – and particularly those that have NHBRC accreditation – will be more reputable. You can also call Master Builders or other associations for referrals. Freebie publications such as *Home Talk* (distributed with newspapers) and online databases like Profinder (www.profinder.co.za) are an excellent resource.

Plan B: interrogate family and friends. Anyone who is prepared to make a referral will presumably only do so based on personal experience with that builder. You'll find that it's not so easy to get referrals. Even when they are forthcoming, that doesn't guarantee a happy outcome: a friend passed on the name of Brilliant Bathroom Person for me to call; eight weeks later, I was still waiting for the quote. It seems to be a peculiar industry trait that people will come and spend three hours on site measuring – at no charge – and then fail to actually draw up the quote. **Tip: Not all quotes are free. Check first.**

Plan C: Ambush people who are browsing in the décor section of the bookshop. Have they renovated? What have they learnt? Do the same at the tile shop or bathroom shop. It is the best way to learn. There's no sales pitch involved, and they are not going to gain anything by recommending a product, builder or artisan to you.

Some professionals start off well and then fizzle out like a tired battery. Rudi the Plumber worked beautifully on his pipes. Then after about four weeks he simply did not come back. Why? Who knows? Luckily, he was being paid a daily rate so it was no loss to us and we simply got someone else in to finish the job.

Theoretically, if a contractor belongs to a professional body, you should be able to claim back for negligent and faulty workmanship, but you may become embroiled in costly litigation before you get any compensation. Contractors often work on a first name and cell number basis only. Good luck finding them if they make off with your deposit. **Tip: Don't pay a deposit (other than for items such as rib and block slabs and steel, where you have no choice) and don't pay the builder to pay for materials. Order and pay the suppliers directly.**

Master builders who are fully guaranteed come with a hefty price that many homeowners cannot afford. A friend of mine recently saw a magnificent house with outstanding workmanship – 'the best she had ever seen'. The quote was five times more than the estimate of a so-called bakkie brigade who also came with excellent references, but no backup or guarantees, courtesy of the NHRBC. Outstanding Builder presented her with a detailed quote in which he levied 14% VAT next to every item – from the bricks to the three-inch nails – and then added another 14% to the whole shebang, as well as his professional fee of 25% of the entire building costs, as his proposed fee. My friend's husband, who is an accountant, is still puzzling over the calculations of Outstanding Builder and, needless to say, they will not be proceeding with him. It would be cheaper, they say, to buy a new house.

On the other hand, you may be reading this and mutter that it is far costlier to hire someone in the informal sector if walls fall apart. From a personal perspective, we have had work done by several operators who definitely do not fall within the ambit of any master builder associations, and the work has been first class. I watched with awe as a lovely man, Uncle Salie, crafted our staircase frame, which was later cast with concrete. The carpentry was sheer artistry.

To manage, or not to manage?

This brings us to the critical decision of whether you are going to take on the role of project manager, or whether you are going to hire someone else to do so. Project manager could be the architect, designer, or draughtsperson. You need to define what your project manger will do. Do you want him or her to buy the materials? Do you want them to simply manage the site and check that walls are going up straight? Some project managers will charge between 15 and 25% of the building costs. Others may be paid a fixed rate (per day, week, month) to oversee the operations. Again, I would be very wary of giving someone carte blanche to order materials on my behalf.

One project manager implied that we were being stupid by managing this project ourselves. I beg to differ. Many of us cannot afford to pay someone to manage our home renovations for us. We need to demystify the subject and help each other to find the right people to get the job done.

Whilst it is true that project managers will tell prospective clients that they receive substantial discounts which they pass on to clients, if you are dealing with OPM (other people's money) there is not much of an incentive to keep within a budget. My daughter's teacher bought carpets recently. She went to all the shops herself. Her project manager, who had done the bulk of her house renovations, levied 20% – although he had nothing whatsoever to do with that particular transaction. Good money, if you can get it. Everyone is entitled to be paid a fair wage for their time and labour, but examples like this breed discontent, and understandably so.

Who is an expert?

As to what is required for your renovations, a lot depends on the nature of the work and where you live. If you are building in a marshy area, for example, you may need a geo-technical engineer. You don't need a qualified plumber to fit a new toilet, although it is recommended. Any electrical work will require a qualified and licensed electrician, who must give you a compliance certificate when the work is complete. This is the document that (you hope) confirms the house wiring is safe and correct. It is preferable that electrical and plumbing should be done from underneath the foundations, so you need to get these people on board right from the beginning. Plugs, lighting, computer cabling, and TV points all need to be considered early on (see chapter 2). If you don't, you will face delays while conduit is chased into the walls after it has been completed and plastered.

What's it gonna cost

Costing is the critical issue and it is essential that you do your sums before beginning. You need to factor in rubble removal, which piles up quickly and, lest you incur your neighbour's wrath, needs to be spirited away pronto. We found our guardian rubble angel, Toyer, in the Argus Classifieds. Rubble removal per load varies from R150 to about R550. But the R150 quote is for a small bakkie carrying about a ton; the current competitive mark is around R380 for a 6-ton truck. Be careful to separate rubble from other waste, such as cut-down trees, and make sure that it is accessible for the truck, i.e. on or at the pavement. If it's still piled up in your yard, expect to pay much more.

Get to know your local hardware supplier. They are usually only too happy to help – after all, you're going to buy from them again and again.

Tools of the trade, discounts and incentives

Many builders in the informal sector do not have their own tools – you need to provide them with everything, down to screwdrivers and chisels. Props and other equipment may need to be hired – make sure to factor all these goodies into your budget.

In terms of payment, you can pay a daily rate or job rate or combination thereof. The advantage of a daily rate is that you pay as you go; if the builder disappears, you have not lost anything. The disadvantage is that builders may string out a job that should take three days into three weeks. A good way to counteract the lag effect is to agree with your builder how long the job should take and give a performance bonus if it comes in on target.

Builder's discounts range from 5% to as much as 40%, so ask when ordering. Set up good relationships with your suppliers and they will see you right. We had fantastic service from Zenith for sand and stone and Cape Brick for their products. They often pulled out all the stops and made emergency deliveries late Friday afternoon or on Saturday. Shop around for timber prices – Baltic are good, and don't charge delivery. Federated Timber and Airton Timbers are also first rate. Different branches of Penny Pinchers quote against each other, believe it or not. For wooden doors and windows, we found Mega Doors to be the best.

The name of the game is haggle, haggle, haggle. It's no use arguing with a clerk who cannot discount the price. Seek out the manager and insist on your builder's discount. He (or she) can only say no.

Walk the walk and go shopping

We need to become more like a Mandikwazikonke – Xhosa for 'let-me-know-everything.' It is the opposite of the *schlemiel* (the eternal loskop who blunders about, set up for certain failure). Nurture your inner Mandi. While you are about it, learn words in some of our official eleven languages. When you can't find the word in your own language to describe what you are going through, curse in another vernacular. Better than therapy.

It's a good idea to do a walkabout on site at least three times a day and ask continuously: Do you need anything? How many bricks have you got left? Do you need nails? Are you sure you don't need anything? If there is the slightest pause or hesitation or flicker of doubt, zoom in and interrogate. Or suffer the consequences of schlepping. On one hot December day, I visited

Mica hardware eight times. I counted. Turps, masking tape, three-inch nails. We ran out of everything – but at different times in the day. 'That's nothing,' soothed a salesperson. 'One of my customers has already been in twelve times. We close in ten minutes, so there's no way you'll better that.' I'm not sure whether it made me feel heaps better, or worse. What had they bought, that I had forgotten?

If you are an alert reader, you'll notice that the subject of three-inch nails has come up a lot. 'What is with these three-inch nails?' sighed my friend Adi. 'Whenever I talk to you, you're rushing to buy three-inch nails. Have your builders got a three-inch fetish? Why not four-inch nails or four-centimetre nails?' Am I a philosopher? If three-inch is what they need, that's what they get.

Sometimes they don't tell you what they need. You have to suss it by yourself. Look around you. Ask: do you need anything for those things over there? Oh, you need that stuff in the tin. It is called pink primer? Sure, I'll go to Mica and get more. Ask, ask and ask again. Learn as you go. There's nothing worse than falling behind because your materials are not there, especially if you are paying a daily rate.

Having said all that, don't rush. As our housekeeper Nthabiseng (Rebecca) kept telling us while we were building: '*Thatha ixesha lakho*' (take your time). That may seem like a contradiction, as we keep recommending a constant flow of materials and labour. But within that one must not rush. Build carefully and safely. Always.

Here's another piece of advice: Be flexible and go for the gap. On a few occasions, our team of builders (paid a daily rate) did not pitch. The bakkie broke down. It was someone's birthday and they were partying. Fortuitously, a building was going up next to Greg's offices. The workmanship was good and speedy. Impressed, he approached Chris the Builder. Chris and his team moved in and worked on one end of our house while the first team worked on another.

Tip: If you are under time pressures (most of us are), get more than one crew on site. Look around the neighbourhood. If you see builders working on the weekend, acknowledge their great work ethic and get them.

Would I advise project managing to novices? It depends. Greg has some experience in that this was not the first building project he had undertaken. If you are new to this, you will need help, but if you are lucky enough to find an excellent contractor, he or she will guide you all the way. Once you have handled a few small jobs, you'll gain the confidence and knowledge to tackle a full-on renovation.

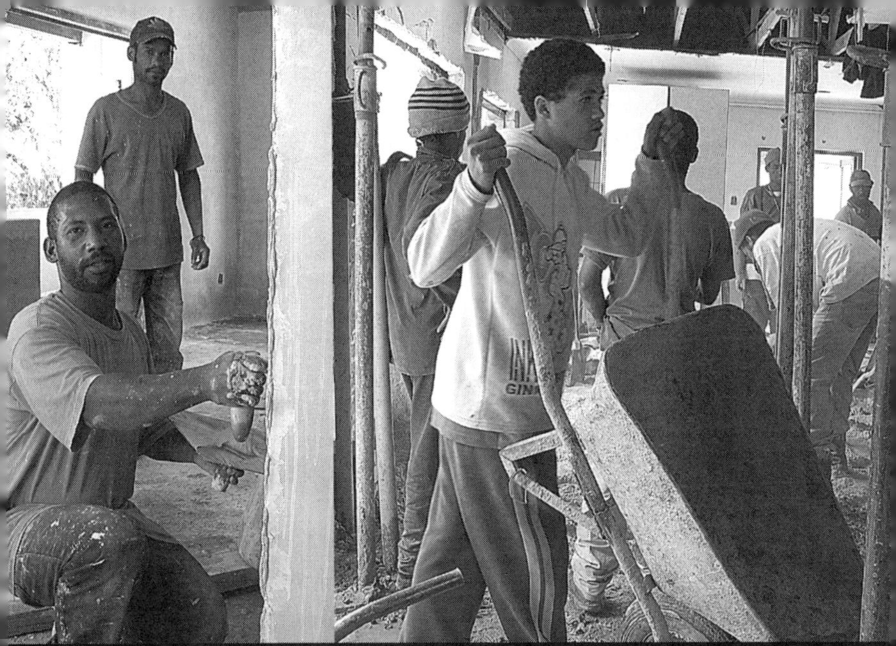

SECTION TWO

Getting on with it

Chapter 5:

Surviving the **wetwork phase**

Wet work has nothing to do with adult movies or the dark side of the CIA, although getting rid of your builder will almost certainly cross your mind. Wet work is commonly used to describe the building process up to but not including the roof, and all finishing work. It includes all stages that involve the use of water.

It goes very fast. Walls are chopped down. Dagga is thrown in every direction. Electricians and plumbers lay cables. Inspectors check the trenches. It is busy and happening. Exciting. All those walls which made the house feel poky and closed in are gone. Wow. And you think to yourself – what on earth were the dire warnings about? This is fun. Were all these people kidding or what? 'Just wait, you'll see,' smirked our friends. 'It gets bad, very bad. And when you get to the finishing ... Ag shame. Be very afraid.'

Their remarks took me back to the first week after Jessie's birth. I gazed at this little angel snuggling at my side and wondered what everyone was on about when they talked of screaming babies. She slept and ate and slept. This was a breeze. 'Just wait, you'll see,' clucked my friends knowingly. 'In a few weeks, she'll realise that this is not a warm and fuzzy womb and it won't be so peaceful.' Sure enough, after a month, little Jess realised she had a good pair of lungs.

Indeed, the hard work of the renovations starts after the basic demolition and new walls have gone up. But first, you have to get past the wet work. Phase one is to get the foundation trenches excavated. Then call your local building inspector to check that the trenches are kosher.

Tip: Save the lovely topsoil that comes out of your trenches to restore your garden when all building has been completed. Keep it away from the building site so it does not get littered with chipped brick, cement, nails and the like, which will render it useless and dangerous to children and pets.

Know your boundaries

If you are building anywhere near or on the boundary line, then it is critical to locate the boundary pegs for your property. Many property disputes start because the pegs (also known as beacons) are not properly identified. Boundary pegs are often hard to find, especially on older properties. They are usually identified as a length of 12mm-thick mild steel reinforcing rod, about half a metre long. They tend to get rusted and don't look important, which is why they get moved by the gardener, thrown away or used by the kids as wickets in their cricket game. If you can't find them, and you have to build on or near your boundary line, you have a problem. Building inspectors will want to see the pegs, and if you can't locate them, you will probably be asked to have the property surveyed to determine exactly where you can build.

Once the inspector gives you the green light for your trenches, you can start to *gooi* concrete. Now, start shopping. It is cheapest to buy your sand and stone in 6 cubic metre loads or more. Ask your builder to estimate how much sand, stone and cement will be required for the foundations. Sand and stone that is delivered to your property is usually dumped onto the pavement (along with bricks). You'll need lots of sand (but it is cheap – about R480 per 6 cubic metre load is about right) for the foundations, any slab work, for mixing dagga, plastering your walls, screeding floors, and putting an underlay for any outside tiled areas. (*See Everybody must get stones …*)

Cement prices are seldom worth shopping around for unless you are prepared to go and collect it yourself. They have been a price-controlled commodity for many years and you may as well buy from your nearest Penny Pinchers, Mica or Federated Timbers. But watch out for delivery charges. Store it in a dry and secure place along with hardware and tools.

Gear up to avoid 'shrinkage'. With 15 or 20 people on site, it is no picnic to watch one team accusing the other of stealing. Appoint one trusted person to be in charge of your stores. Do an inventory each morning and evening to check what has gone out. Order what is required for the next day before 3 pm as many suppliers close their next-day-delivery schedules by 3 pm or 3.30 pm.

Tip: Keep your foundations wet for a day or two after they have been cast by spraying them with water from your hosepipe. The moisture provides for a strengthening of the foundation and this should reduce the likelihood of cracks on your walls a year or so later. If you have the luxury of time on your side, wait a few days for the foundations to set hard, before starting the brickwork.

A team of six with one or two builders should be able to dig almost a hundred linear metres of foundation within about two days – assuming there are no rocks or tree roots in the way.

If you hire a concrete mixer (about R80 a day from Hire Out Tools, who have just about everything you will need), the builders should be able to cast the foundation concrete at the rate of about 60–80 linear metres per day. Your trenches and foundations should be complete within 3–5 days after kickoff.

Your builder will then lay down courses (layers) of standard-size bricks (called imperials) to come up to ground level. That is generally about a day's work. Next they will backfill the foundations with soil. Now is the time to buy your doorframes and windows; within a day or two after the completion of the foundations, your builder will be putting up the walls and will need the

Everybody must get stones ...

Sand, Stone and Cement – also known as aggregates – don't come cheap. So don't buy cheap. If the price sounds too good to be true, then it probably is.

All sands are not equal: Plasterers will complain about sand quality, and rightly so. But the sand for your fill and foundations isn't all that critical. Different loads will have different colours. It is, after all, a natural product.

Stone comes in different sizes: 19 mm is 'normal' concrete size. Smaller sizes will give greater compaction (less air in the gaps). If you are ordering, make sure you get the correct size. It's an expensive product, so shop around.

Don't overstock cement: Unless you can store in a secure dry place near to site. If you are going to be using huge amounts, then shop around, you may save yourself a good few hundred.

windows and frames to fix into the structure as the brickwork goes up.

Ensure that you have ordered windows and doorframes at least two to three days before you need them. Shop around for specials.

Tip: Beware the rough work carpenter who says he/she can hang your doors when your building is complete. Door hanging is an art and specialist carpenters charge around R400 per door. That's a whole lot of cash if you have lots of doors to hang, so factor that into your budget.

Tip: Wooden doorframes and windows come treated, but should be completely painted with 2 or 3 coats of TimberCare or similar product, before being fixed into place – this will extend their life by many years. Metal doorframes are treated against rust, but should also be painted with Hammerite or similar product before being fixed into place. This will minimise rusting of the frames in years to come.

This is the part when everything seems to be going quickly. Wait. The finishes cause the *tzoris* (Yiddish for stress) – but that we get to later.

Up to speed?

The speed of the building process is directly related to the availability of materials and amount of labour on site. A bricklayer usually works with two assistants, one of whom is fetching and preparing bricks while the other is mixing cement. The more hands, the faster you build. If you are paying a daily rate, pull in extra labour to speed up the process. It is at this foundation phase that you must get your plumber to lay down any waste lines. If you are extending out, a slab floor will need to be cast, and your electrician must lay conduit lines before the slab concrete is cast.

Vital tip: Take photos to help you remember where your electrical conduit pipes are before they get covered up, so you don't hit them if you have to drill or chase channels at a later stage.

Plug circuits usually come up from the floor and lights from the ceiling above. A plumber needs to come and lay out copper conduit pipe for water supply to baths, basins, loos, etc., but the supply pipes (hot and cold) usually run from the geyser, through the roof and down the walls to the taps.

As soon as your plans are passed, get your designer/architect to get a roof truss design prepared and get quotes. Roof trusses can take up to three weeks to be manufactured so this is an order that needs to be fast-tracked.

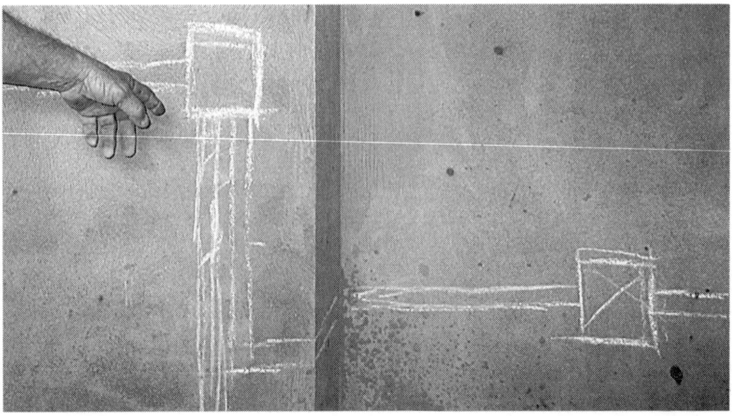

The problem is that the manufacturer will almost always want to take final measurements on site, once the walls are up. A bit of a catch 22. Your builder could be up to roof height within ten days of starting, so at least get the basic quotes approved and paid for (you have to pay upfront for trusses). Ask the roof truss people to quote on all necessary timber for the roof structure including wall plates, tile battens and fascia boards, but not your ceiling battens (*see Battens – why wait?*).

Once your builder has started, you'll need to keep him/her fed with a regular supply of bricks, sand and cement, as well as brick-force and tie-wires. Brick-force is a roll of galvanised metal available in different widths (depending on wall thickness) and is placed every third course to reinforce the walls. It looks a bit like a thin ladder, all made of wire and rolled up. It is almost always specified on plans, and for your peace of mind don't try any shortcuts to save a few rands. Tie-wires are butterfly-shaped galvanised metal wire loops which hold the cavity walls together. If you see a structure without these wires going in, start worrying. Your building will not be structurally sound.

Your builder will require lintels to go over external doors and frames, to support brickwork above. Some internal doorways may also require support.

Once you are near roof height, you need galvanised hoop iron, which is cemented into the brickwork, four courses of bricks below the top of the wall. The hoop iron is later nailed to the roof trusses to hold the roof down.

Measuring time – in metres

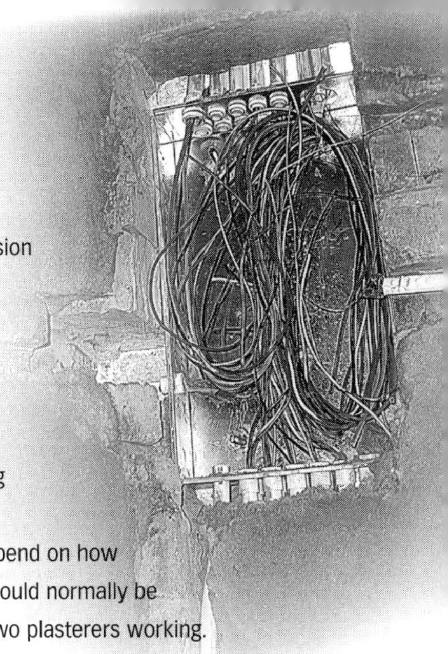

As an indicator of time, a two-room extension with say 60 square metres of new space will involve about 24 linear metres of foundations, because one wall (the pre-existing structure) is usually already there. Using a team of six or seven people, it should take not more than 8 to 10 working days to have everything up to roof height. Plastering internally and externally will depend on how many windows and doors you have, but would normally be completed within two to four days, with two plasterers working.

Before plastering, get the electrician to grind out all channels to lay conduit for the four types of wiring usually needed: power for plugs, power for lights, TV, and telephone. Different wiring takes different diameter conduit: normal power in 20 mm, the others in at least 25 mm. Computer cabling, in our view, is going to be redundant – within a few years we'll be in a wireless world.

Tip: Don't buy 90° bends for PVC conduit. Your electrician should be able to bend the PVC pipe with a coil of spring. Moulded 90° bends are expensive, and you will then also need to buy couplings.

Get the builder to build 'square and level'. The builder must use a long level and a large set square and make sure that all walls are straight and, where there is a perpendicular, that it is at 90° and not a thumbsuck. Don't be shy. If it looks *skeef*, it must come down. If it is the builder's mistake, then penalties

Battens – why wait?

Generally you will buy your ceiling battens along with your ceilings; by that stage of the process, you can make an accurate calculation of the amount of materials required for the ceiling. Ceiling battens may vary widely in length; if you buy all your timber at the beginning, you may well end up with wastage. Example: if you were to buy all your battens say in 6m lengths, you may find that you only need short little lengths of 1.8m or 2m in the toilet. There's nowhere to use the other 4 metres – other than as a stake to drive through the builder who is driving you crazy. We reckon that it's best to buy your ceilings and battens once all your roofing timber, plumbing and electrical work in the roof area – other than the final installation of lights – is completed.

should apply. Skew walls will come back to haunt you when the tiles look terrible, and cupboards don't fit.

As soon as the roof trusses are on, you need your A19 compliance certificate. The roof tiles/sheets and ceilings cannot be fitted until the A19 has been issued. It is your assurance that the roof is structurally sound, properly braced and is unlikely to be ripped off in the next south-easter. I never found out if there is an A18 or an A20. But the A19 is what you need. (*See What's the A19?*)

A19 inspectors come to site and check trusses. They climb up and have a good look, tapping and prodding anything that looks wonky. If everything is fine and you have the fee ready, you'll receive the A19 certificate. If not, they'll return and do another check. Twenty-four-hour notice is required to tell them you are ready for them to inspect.

In terms of roof covering, avoid exotic tiles that may be difficult to obtain in ten years' time when a few of them break. Slate, thatch and various coverings are other options. The most cost-effective is long-span galvanised IBR sheeting (inverted box rib). Many suppliers sell the same product – shop around. It is important – if you can afford it – to use the higher quality (0.05/275 gram) zinc IBR which has a higher percentage of zinc in it and will therefore last longer.

Before you pay your roofing contractor, and before the ceilings are in, wait for it to rain solidly. If that does not happen, go mad with your hosepipe. Is the roof properly flashed and sealed where it comes up against parapet walls? If you stand underneath the roof at midday and you can see bits of sun, then you can see where it is going to leak. Light shines through the holes. It is as simple as that.

What's the A19?

In terms of the national building regulations, an A19 completion certificate is required for all 'rationally designed systems'. Eddie Bock at the Institute of Timber Construction (ITC) head office in Johannesburg explains: 'Rational refers to a nail-plated timber roof truss which is rationally designed – i.e. designed by calculation, an engineered product.' Tracking down the number for the A19 is not easy. It took us several phone calls to find the national contact numbers. Several building associations said, 'What? We don't know about that, your builder must do it for you.' Duh, we are the builder, whom must we call? Dunno. The ITC seem to know all about building regulations with obscure names. Call them and find out more (see page 98).

Seeing through the glaze

As soon as your window frames have been inserted, phone around for glazing quotes. Standard 3 mm glass is usually used for window panes of up to about one square metre. Above that and you must use 4 mm, or even 6 mm. Ask the glass company to cut the glass but do not install until all walls have been plastered. It's no fun cleaning cement off glass.

A lovely way to finish off interior walls is to skim walls (and ceilings) using Cretestone. Skimming in this context means 'smoothing' and has nothing to do with what unscrupulous project managers do when ordering materials. When mixed with water, Cretestone forms a fine, clay-like mixture, which is then plastered over the raw cement and gives a very smooth finish. Some people leave the Cretestone as the final finish and apply a sealer. Only skim when all other subcontracting work (plumbing, electrical) has been completed.

It took us roughly seven weeks to rip our house apart and rebuild it to the point where we were into the finishing phase. We added about 70 square metres. Initially it looked like a house of ruins. I felt emotionally freaked out. Hey, this was our house they were breaking apart. We are so used to computer simulation: take a wall away, put another one up – it's easy as pie. The reality is very different and involves noise, dust and a demolition squad with hammers and mallets bashing your walls down. Later it started to take shape, and then began the hard part – finishing.

More is more

Rather have too many than too few:

1. Plug points in each room.
2. Plug points in your kitchen.
3. Taps for your scullery/washing room.
4. Garden taps.
5. Outside lights, especially for pathways.
6. Spare electrical and phone conduits, clearly marked.
7. Light switches that are two-way, especially where you may enter/exit important rooms from different areas at night. You don't want to be groping around the kitchen when you come in through the garage, looking for the switch, which is at the doorway to your lounge.
8. Spare roof tiles, floor tiles, and just about anything else that comes in a batch where matching colour in future will be impossible.
9. Words of thanks to any supplier who delivers goods to site. The loads they are moving for you are often hard and heavy.
10. Spare Cokes and even maybe a cold beer if it's a hot summer day and the guys are mixing concrete.
11. Nice things to say to your builder. Money isn't the only good motivator. Give compliments where they are due – they go a long way.
12. Moments of joy at what you are creating, and your good fortune that you can.

Consider also

Pest control – Watch out for things that go munch in the night
Be careful of imported natural timbers that may not have been treated for beetles and other goggas that can literally eat through beams and de-stabilise the structure, or even bring it crashing down.

Chapter 6:

Selecting paint – by staking out other people's rooms

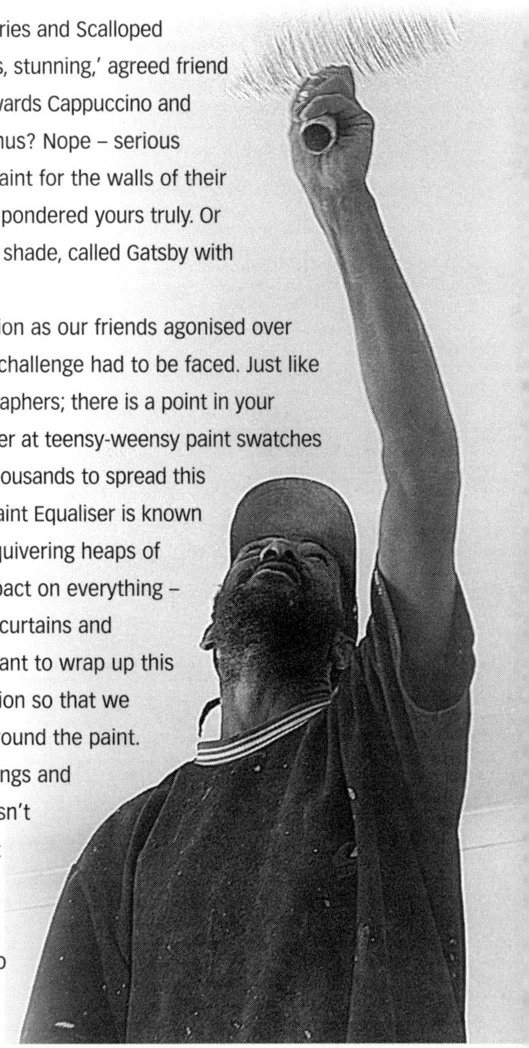

'I am so happy with my French Fries and Scalloped Potatoes,' gushed my friend. 'Yes, stunning,' agreed friend number two, 'but I'm leaning towards Cappuccino and Crème Brulée.' Dinner party menus? Nope – serious discussion over the colours of paint for the walls of their homes. What about Slap Chips? pondered yours truly. Or how about a special Cape Town shade, called Gatsby with *Smoer-Snoek*?

We had watched in trepidation as our friends agonised over paint colour. We knew that this challenge had to be faced. Just like parallax gets panoramic photographers; there is a point in your renovation when you have to peer at teensy-weensy paint swatches and make a decision to spend thousands to spread this liquid on your walls. The Great Paint Equaliser is known to reduce strong individuals to quivering heaps of jelly. Colour of the walls will impact on everything – from your choice of tiles to the curtains and cupboards. For us it was important to wrap up this decision early on in the renovation so that we could build our other finishes around the paint. Others choose their floor coverings and work from that direction. It doesn't matter, but you do have to start somewhere and then consider your finishes in relation to one another. Do the floor tiles talk to the wall or do they scream at each other?

For our interior walls, we wanted a white that was not pure white but did not look yellow under artificial light. We wanted the paint to act as a backdrop for our home, against which we could project our ideas and, if necessary – money permitting – perhaps add focal walls of colour at a later stage.

When white is right

Ten years ago when we moved into our house, choosing white paint was a breeze. White was white. We had a choice of basic white, crème or eggshell or something to that effect. Eggshell went on the walls and white on the ceilings. The original paint (Plascon) is in pretty good shape, but with our renovation and ripped-out walls it was time to paint.

Now, there is just too much choice. Suede finish. Glaze look. Scumble look. Floor paint, tile paint, fireplace paint, container paint. There is apparently a new technology that imparts fragrance into the paint. Lemon Yellow smells of lime. The perfume doesn't last very long – a few weeks maybe – but is said to replace the chemical odour of newly applied paint. It does not seem to be available yet in this country.

Then I was saved. A colleague suggested that I go and see an 'essay of white' at the Cape Cadogan, a sexy little boutique hotel in Upper Union Street. It was a gloomy, drizzly Monday morning – a good one to go paint spotting. After about five seconds I knew that this was the colour for me. Loved the name: White Canvas (also Plascon). Loved the sense of calm that the colour evoked. (Essential for a family of A-type personalities who need calming.) I returned later that day to see how it fared in the midday sun. Lekker. What intrigued me about this colour is that it looks different in various rooms depending on the light sources and furnishings.

How does my butt – I mean, façade – look in this colour?

Lucky for me, during my morning visitation the interior designer David Strauss was at the Cadogan for a meeting. Strauss, I was told, is responsible for the design of the hotel. I pounced. Would he please reveal all in the fine art of choosing paint? It is all about context, he replied. Recently he chose Lemon Chicken for an Afrikaans school. It was sublime. The Cape Cadogan, he explained, was an Edwardian building. 'We wanted to create a contemporary feel. People don't want to stay in a museum.' When the hotel's development began, the boudoir look was in so they were going against the décor grain. 'White wasn't in. Now there are hundreds of whites – malted milk, Grecian white, lamb's wool – but this was right for this property.'

People should be careful of whites that veer towards the yellow spectrum, and look at how these are altered by artificial light. White Canvas, he told me, gets its kick because of a dash of yellow, red, and black.

Decorating tip: Use a gloss white on ceilings. It gives an illusion of height. Paint a wall and see how your eye reacts. Don't choose a million colours. Create a backdrop and use your accessories to ring the changes. Always select colour for your space and not according to trends.

Right, I was sorted. White Canvas for interior walls, 'normal' white for ceilings. Would Greg agree? He accompanied me to the Cadogan on a Sunday afternoon at 5 pm. Typical male: took him two seconds to decide – yes. We did not consider other brands because we had such a good experience with Plascon, which comes with a 7-year guarantee (and it is good to know that you can always get more of the same colour – keep the code on the tin and they will mix it).

Then we needed to decide which type of paint to buy. Go for Cashmere, I was told at the hardware shop. Now I was really confused. Cashmere refers here not to the colour but the type of interior paint. It is apparently tops: extremely hard-wearing, drip resistant, tough against children's hands, and washable.

I logged onto www.plascon.co.za and found a nifty link to help estimate how much paint to buy. Type in details about room dimensions etc. and the programme punches out an estimate. Most hardware shops will not take paint back, so you need to get your figures sorted. An operator from Plascon's Advisory Service told me that paint technicians do home visits (no charge) and advise how much paint is required.

One of the interesting features on the site is a 'visualiser' which allows you to download software and input a digital image of your room (demo only – the full version is sold at hardware shops). Try red on that dining room. The programme 'colours' your walls. Too dramatic? Try another colour.

It's clever, but I still don't think there is anything to beat seeing a *stuk* of paint *in situ*, in real spaces where there are curtains and blinds, and you can see how it has weathered in high traffic areas like passages. Our home is now open on the first Sunday of every month for all to check out the paint. Lemon and poppyseed muffins and coffee included. Only kidding, but I think we all need a real version of virtual reality shopping.

Building is just another word for shopping – become a local yokel

In terms of the virtual reality domain, we have been disappointed at the poor standard of décor-related sites – if they exist at all. Many suppliers have show-rooms but refer you to the nearest retailer. This means two trips' worth of petrol and time. It would be great to reduce the schlep work by visiting a website to get an idea of what is up for grabs. We were surprised at how few suppliers are open on a Sunday. At best, places are open until 1 pm on a Saturday. On Sunday, besides Mica Hardware and CTM, almost everything is shut down.

From a service perspective, for the most part we found that shopping at smaller operators was more productive. They generally try harder. Their ranges may be smaller but they have considered their stock more carefully than their (larger) opposition. If they don't have it, they'll source it. Some of our best finds were through the Yellow Pages or through the community newspapers. We found a lovely shop, Dynamic Bathrooms in Diep River, because of an ad for a toilet we saw in a community spreadsheet.

Going for the botox effect – please, no wrinkles in our paint

Paints are carefully formulated products, and if you want quality, be prepared to pay a little more. Look around – many 5-year-old spec homes look shabby because they were finished with inferior paint. Then look at a 30-year-old home that still looks good.

Along with tiling, you'll discover that everyone and their Oom can paint. Barriers to entry = 1 *kwas* (paintbrush) and a roller, so it's a crowded market. Get wise to some jargon with a quick test. Ask: how much universal undercoat will you need for the raw plaster? If they give you an amount, tell them that their services are not required; the correct answer is none. The first coat is plaster primer, which is alkaline resistant. It gets soaked up by the walls. It's expensive, but if you don't use it, your paint job will need redoing in a few years.

On wood, use what is commonly called pink primer (because that's its colour). After the primer, lay down your universal undercoat, and when all is dry, your final coat.

Internally, if you are repainting, you may be able to skip the universal under-coat, but it is a barrier coat essential to painting any area where there was previously a different type of paint to the one you now intend finishing with.

Three layers may seem like overkill, but when you're paying nearly R1,000 per 20 litres of good-quality final coat, would you seriously risk redoing it in a few years because you thought you might get away with just a basic undercoat?

When painting internally, mineral turpentine can be added to almost any primer coat in the ratio of about 1:5 (i.e. 1 x 750 ml bottle turps to 5 litres paint), which will increase the absorption into the surface. This is very useful, particularly on raw cement or Cretestone. When painting external walls, do the woodwork first. Any wood sealer that splashes or drips onto the plaster can then be painted over, whereas if you paint first, especially with white, it's a pain to get the stuff off, and it never really comes clean.

Only paint when all the grinding, tiling and carpentry work is complete. Dust is the enemy. Be patient and schedule everything in its own time. Grind, cut and sand outside, far from the windows and doors (and keep those closed as you approach the end, to keep out the dust).

Buy a huge sheet of DPC plastic to use as a drop sheet. DPC is cheap, will save hours of clean-up and can be used later as an underlay on outside paving, or lining for fishponds.

Common sense is to be followed: start with the roof paint, then work down. If repainting the roof, make sure it is thoroughly cleaned beforehand. Climb up the ladder and check. Paint between about 10 am and 4 pm, allowing the external areas to be dry before you start, and allow to set before the evening dew.

Internally, start with the ceilings and work down. Ceilings will often be plain white, and usually the cornice is included in that colour. Make sure that all cracks between cornice and ceiling are sealed using painter's mate (acrylic sealer, not silicone), which is marvellous stuff. This will stop dust falling through the ceiling in years to come.

When painting externally, think wind. Make sure your painter doesn't work in a howling south-easter that will carry the fine mist which the roller spits onto your neighbour's shiny new black BMW. And if paint does end up where it shouldn't, then get the correct solvent to remove it. Don't guess! You may think that lacquer thinners will work, but it may also destroy the very thing you're trying to clean.

Most important of all: don't rush it. Yes, you're tired, and desperate to get your life back to normal. Plaster takes time to dry, Cretestone looks dry but isn't, and the end result of a rushed paint job is a botched job. That's why most paint instructions recommend that you wait up to 4 weeks before painting.

Chapter 7:

Get your dreams out of the closet – **cupboards to platz over**

Marie-Henri Beyle was a 19th-century author who went by the pseudonym of Stendhal. On a maiden visit to Florence in 1817, Beyle was overcome by the art in the city and wrote about his experiences. In the late 1970s, an Italian psychiatrist observed this strange but commonplace phenomenon, whereby tourists to Florence would become out of breath, swoon, hallucinate and faint from pure exhilaration at the beauty around them. She named the condition Stendhal's syndrome.

When I read about Stendhal's I thought: Hmmm, sounds familiar. For example, I felt faint, dizzy, out of breath and overcome with euphoria when I beheld a wooden slab sprayed in white high gloss by Imraan Samodien in Diep River. I could not believe that anything could be so beautiful: smooth, shiny, no edges or joins. I carried the wood around for a week and showed everyone I knew.

You are probably thinking, this woman is crazy to go into raptures over a paint finish for her kitchen cupboards. In order for you to understand my Stendhalic euphoria over Imraan's high gloss, let's wind the tape back and give the background to this story.

Sourcing cupboards for our house was an undertaking that left us reeling in disappointment. Many manufacturers produce boards that look fantastic in catalogues, but the reality is often very different.

You'll need to get with the jargon on this subject. There are three types of wood available for cupboards: solid natural timber (most expensive); supa-wood (also quite pricy); and chipboard. Supa-wood is almost like solid wood but is a manufactured product. Cupboards, even the most expensive ones, are almost always built from a carcass of chipboard. The internal panels, the bits that you don't see, are made of the stuff. It's called Bison board, Magnaboard,

Magnalam, Bisonlam, SonaeBoard, etc. and it's all quite similar. It's chipboard that is pressed together and then lined on the outside with different types of finish. The boards are supplied in standard size of about 1830 x 2730 mm. They are all 16 mm thick. The bench tops are similarly produced, except they are 32 mm thick, and usually 600 mm wide (standard width for a bench top) and either 2700 mm or 3500 mm long.

Once the cupboard design is finalised, a cutting schedule is prepared, and sent to the board supplier. They take these big sheets and cut them up into smaller pieces: the doors, sides, front and side panels for drawers. When you examine the boards in the showroom, they look great, with big smooth panels of sophisticated engineering. The problem: the flat panel looks nice, but the leading edge, the part you see when you open the door, is rough brown stuffed chipbase. That edge has to be sealed somehow.

The cheapest system is to have it 'edged' with a strip of 16 mm veneer glued onto the leading edge. It can result in sharp corners and doesn't last long at all. If you have ever seen kitchen cupboards that look all rough at the bottom edge, the reason is simple: water, coffee, tea and soup spill down the face of the cupboard, and that moisture gets between the front panel and the glued edge. That moisture hits the chipbase, and ugly swelling wood spills out.

Several systems have been devised to overcome this problem, such as 'impact edging'. This involves a thick piece of plastic (coloured to match the

board surface), rather than a thin veneer. It comes in 1, 2 or 3 mm. When done correctly, it's far neater and sturdier than normal edging. It also costs up to twice the price, as the board has to be carefully cut to accommodate the size and then passed through a special machine, which glues the edging on. It then has to be trimmed and cleaned off.

Mouldings and wraps

There are also moulded door edges, which come in a variety of profiles. Whilst you can't see the join line, the edges are often quite sharp. We were very keen on moulded doors but the cost was prohibitive. By that stage we had made some basic choices. We had decided to do our bedroom and office cupboards the laminate way, but were keen to have a nicer finish for our white kitchen cupboards. Then we heard about 'wrapped doors', which sounded like the answer. We were told that the doors are shrink-wrapped with wood laminate so that there are no joins. It is like covering your doors with plastic and sealing it with those heat machines they use at Pick 'n Pay to clamp the plastic wrap over your fruit salad container, ensuring that it doesn't leak. The vinyl process with no seams is fantastic for kitchens and bathrooms – in effect there is no leading edge, no joins, nowhere for the water to get in and cause all that trouble.

After the sales spiel, we were ready to max out the credit card. We wanted white but the white in the wrap looks pimply – like it had a fine rash of cellulite. We eventually selected a sublime champagne colour. Then we opened the cupboard doors in a show-room and saw the insides: white melamine. Imagine wrapping a book as a gift, finding that you only have enough for the front and sides and using white paper for the back. To us, it looked incomplete; the wrap only goes about 50 mm around the edge, which, in our view, looks awful. Even if you choose white, you have a very nicely finished white wrapped outer door, and plain white chipboard inside with a nasty little join line – like a panty line that won't go away. Given the price of wrapped doors, it hardly seemed worth it. Once again, we learnt how important it is to view something *in situ* – either in a showroom or in someone's home. I would have freaked if we had paid premium price and only discovered the design flaw (as we see it) when the kitchen person was installing.

For us, it was back to the white melamine for the kitchen; but looking around at other people's edges, we were not hopeful. The manufacturers we dealt with do not guarantee their work. Attention to detail and quality control are not high on the priority list. It seems you just have to be happy with wood pulp peeping here and there, bits of glue, and spaces where the laminate edging doesn't fit.

Beautiful but tough

We had toyed with the idea of high gloss (also known as Chinese lacquer) but all the samples we had seen had shown up fingermarks and chipped easily just from handling. Then Mike, our cabinetmaker, our saviour, referred us to Imraan. And this is how I ended up having my Stendhal syndrome moment. Imraan's vivacious and very glam wife Zulfa called me to collect my sample.
I swooned in excitement when presented with this magnificent piece of glossy white wood. After seeing jagged melamine edging, it was a moment of pure bliss to view something so perfect.

Imraan asked: 'Tell me, is your kitchen a busy area. Do you use it a lot?' What a question! We are Jewish and food is our calling. We love our kitchen. We use it hard. If that is the case, Imraan suggested, we should reconsider the high gloss. Although it is paint used on yachts and is hardy, a matt or satin finish is more resilient. It is also easier to retouch a ding or mark, whereas with the high gloss, the whole piece must be redone.

Imraan uses Plascon for matt and satin and says the paint is therefore fully guaranteed by them. We appreciated his honesty. There is nothing worse than spending a lot of money only to find out at a later stage that it was the wrong way to go. We wish everyone was as forthcoming about function and suitability and not so quick to tell you what you want to hear (as in: the gloss is divine, will be fine, no of course it won't chip even if your kids use the kitchen as a hip hop practice studio).

For the kitchen doors and sides we chose the white satin finish, and impact edging for the interior shelves. The matt or satin also happens to be half the price of the gloss, so we scored on the financial side.

For the bedrooms, we wanted a warmer tone than white, which we felt would be too sterile for banks of cupboards. We chose red alder with impact edging, hoping to recreate a sense of Japanese screening. Very Zen.

How did it turn out? Overall we are happy. Credit must go to Mike's workmanship; doors close properly, hinges are concealed. The drawer runners are a dream. For the first time, we actually have closets we can be proud of.

The finishing is not as good as we would like, and yes, we are fussy. I just don't think the board manufacturers care – quick buck, volume business, and since you have to pay up-front, you have just about zero recourse. Use wood filler to hide the edges, they told us. Thanks a lot: that was your job, to finish the edges.

Tip: Go to the factory before you pay, and get a sample made up – properly, as neat as possible. Then tell them they must produce everything to that standard, or it gets rejected, and get them to sign on that condition.

Then, and here's the tough part, inspect and reject ruthlessly. We were under time pressure and needed to fast-track the process. If you can, don't rush.

If we had our time again, we would build the cupboard carcasses, live without the doors, and at a later stage – money available – get sprayed supa wood doors. The beauty of supa-wood, or solid doors, is that you can change the colour (spray or paint) without having to replace the doors.

Consider the following figures but please do not go into shock: If you have a half-million to spend renovating your house, and you're redoing your cupboards, then you'll probably blow R100K (yes, onehundredthousand) on your cupboards – at least. And we are not talking solid wood doors, just melamine. We got quotes from a kitchen company that clicked in at R90K – just for the kitchen. If you want solid wood, with the joints dovetailed and perfectly lined up, then add on a lot more. If you go with a cabinetmaker like we did, you not only save but also get bespoke cupboards, as they like to say in the UK décor magazines. It does mean a considerable amount of work from homeowners – measuring, sourcing and buying the boards and hinges.

Whatever you choose, try to avoid the mistake that so many make – they spend fortunes on renovating and then install awful cupboards. Why bother renovating if the end result looks cheap? Cupboards get hammered. The kitchen, bathroom, children's rooms – the poor cupboards go bang the whole day. Cupboards which are chipped and badly edged make a place look tired.

Set up a closet fund

Here's the Big Tip: Before you begin, put aside money for the cupboards, paint and carpets, and then work your way backwards and work out your building costs.

A *skeef* wall can be rectified by plastering and skimming, but awful cupboards and carpets stick out like awful cupboards and carpets. Take your cupboard money and put it in a separate account or, better still, give that money to someone you trust, who will not crack under pressure. No matter how much you cajole and beg and plead, they must not give you your money until you are ready to pay for your cupboards. You may not misappropriate the cupboard fund for fancy cornices or other *tzatzkes* (miscellaneous clutter).

We were at the 80% phase. Translated, that means we were approaching the nearly, nearly finished stage. Most but not all cornices were in place. Same with the tiles, the cupboards and the outside paving. The ceiling contractor had gone walkabout. He said he would return in time for the kitchen assembly which was due to begin in a few days. He had another urgent job. Everyone's job is urgent but we won't go into that. Suffice to say: he did return – two days later than he had said he would. We were relieved.

As for the breathing exercises to alleviate Stendhal's: there aren't any. At least, none that I know of. Ahh, the agony and ecstasy of building…

TEL: 510 5500/4/5
tiles
51 PAARDEN EILAND
CLOSED

SECTION THREE

Finishing

Chapter 8:

On-site sibling rivalry – **or how to keep the peace**

What to Expect When You Are Expecting is a classic text that many pregnant women read. My friend Jenny, who gave birth recently, remarked that this book is excellent because it prepares you for everything – particularly for what can go wrong. There is no equivalent manual, that I know of, for renovating and how one should orchestrate on-site dynamics.

Picture the following scenario: You walk into your lounge and your children are doing something unmentionable. 'But, ma, dad said we could,' they chant. Their timing is impeccable: they nab you when you are tired, flustered, and not really listening. It doesn't sound right. But it's been a long day. Later on it's time for the truth. Dad is horrified. How could you be so naïve, so gullible? Who is the boss around here?

When contractor one sanguinely tells you that he is carrying out spouse's orders to do something which sounds incredibly stupid, you blithely say, 'Oh, alright.' His timing is impeccable: you are worn out, distracted. Spouse is horrified. How could you be so naïve, so gullible? Who is the boss around here?

It gets worse. In the background, I hear the one builder yelling, 'Ou Gat, Ou Gat!' I think he is referring to me and my absolute naivety. Turns out that that is his name. Most of them have learnt on the job from their father/uncle/brother/friend. It is every man for himself (there has not been one woman) and here a spade is a spade. It is not a place for euphemisms.

Tell the contractors that they get their instructions from one person. Establish who the Boss is and then stick to the pecking order. Constantly check with your spouse and make sure that what is being done is correct. It may sound easy but when you are both juggling work and building 24/7, you are not exactly engaging in meaningful discussions with each other. The sub-text here: relationships take strain. Let's be honest.

Building is all about timing, as has been noted several times in this book. You need to get your orders for next-day deliveries and make sure that there is a flow of materials onto the site (see chapter 5 on the wetwork stage). What hasn't been discussed is the time frame of the entire operation. You don't want to be racing to the finishing line, like we did, in the first weeks of December. Half this town shuts down from the first week of December. The other half … well, let's not talk about the other half. Just make sure you avoid them. Orders are closed for blinds, kitchen tops, and so on. We made it, but too close for comfort.

'Ag, shame,' commiserated our friends, 'you're heading for Builders' Holiday.' As it happened, BH was not the problem. Builders in the formal industry accrue their leave so that they can take a paid holiday, which traditionally begins on the 16th. For those in the informal industry, this is not an issue: no work, no pay. With unemployment rates, there is no shortage of people to work. The problem is that suppliers are either shutting down or have simply run out of stock. It is frightening how much building industry material is imported. 'Oh, sorry, we're waiting for a container – be here next year,' one hears all the time. Next year might be only two weeks away, but when you are building, time is money. And we wanted our house back.

Building on time – start before mid-year

If you are contemplating a major renovation, then this is possibly, as they say in academia, the seminal chapter in this book. Want to gut half your house and add on a bit here and there, like we have? Start the process now. Cut your annual leave. Do not have a holiday. Postpone the summer.

In your spare time – on the weekends and public holidays – find a draughtsperson/architect/designer who is prepared to work with you on your plans. Hash out those plans and re-work them. Be ready to submit by January. We were told that it would take 6–8 weeks to get our plans through Council. It took us 10. The process was slowed down because our application was incomplete and was sent back to us, which delayed the process. If we had needed permission from our neighbours or departures from Council, the process might have been delayed even further. Processing varies in the different municipalities and may also be affected by the number of applications in the system.

We completed our wet work in seven weeks but we did this with two teams of builders. Other people we know have taken six months for similar jobs, and then needed another three months for finishing. Do the math: you'll see that for major renovations to be safe, rather than sorry, you don't want to begin building later than May. This allows you time to do the wet work and complete finishes without the end of the year rush.

Talking of which, shops have sales during the festive season and it's a good idea to shop for your finishes then. Buy toilets, basins, taps and other accessories. During the finishing stages, you'll suddenly need everything at once and be running around trying to buy tiles, handles, plates for plugs and lights all at the same time.

It was during the finishing stage that we really appreciated being in our digs across the road. You don't have to get into your car and drive to the site. You are on the spot. Contractors can start early and work late or work over weekends. More importantly, you are there all the time – watching.

Our rented house looked like a builder's warehouse: tiles, hardware and plumbing parts scattered around, a section for hardware and tools, power tools, a paint section. It helped us keep control of the many smaller items used on site that can easily go walkabout. Even so, we just couldn't seem to account for a couple of taps, a showerhead and a few paintbrushes.

Handling the extras – there will be plenty

You will also have to deal with extras you had not budgeted for, like door handles. Until we renovated I had never looked at the door handles. You could have put me on a witness stand, got me to swear an oath and I would not have been able to testify about their dimensions, colour or shape. Then I had an OMG (omigod) moment of mammoth proportions when I saw the stainless steel door handles in my friend Tanya's newly renovated house. Had to have them. Put them onto the new doors we had purchased for the extra additions. Guess what? The old handles in our home looked hideous. Had to replace the lot. Crunch time for that lovely little budget of ours. Much to the bemusement of Ryan Linde and staff of Cape Handle Bar in Wynberg, I initially bought three handles, and then returned and purchased three more, and so it went until I had handled the house. I had some birthday money from friends that I was going to use to buy jewellery. Instead, I bought handles.

Some of our old locks in the house worked with the new handles and others needed to be replaced. Another expense. Check when purchasing: are the must-have handles compatible with existing locks (the part inside the door)? Are the handles compatible with the old doors (hollow, solid, etc.)? In that vein, will the doors fit the frames?

Before we began renovating, we were advised that when estimating building costs, one should add 20% and then double that figure. This seemed excessive to me but I can now see that this is not a ridiculous claim.

Highly recommended: plan your renovation a year in advance. If you are salaried employees, bank your annual leave and arrange that your leave will commence the day that the building starts. Ask if they will give you an additional week's leave and then, for the month or so for the finishes, get your spouse to arrange that his/her annual leave commences roughly a month after yours; you then have two months for supervising in paid leave. You are going to need to be present when you may have five or six contractors on site. They have to wait in line to begin their job and sibling rivalry is nothing in relation to the friction that goes on between professionals of different persuasions and worldviews working in a hot and dusty environment. Sparks fly and it is best for you to be there.

Watch out for contracts not worth the paper they are written on

Gina of Parklands learned this to her cost. She was not able to be at home while minor renovations were taking place, and says that the job was botched. No worries, she thought. It stated on her invoice that the builder is a member of a professional body which is supposed to cover homeowners in the event of things going wrong. Gina called the association. 'Sorry,' they told her, 'we cannot help you because you did not build from the ground up. We do not cover renovations, only a new build.' Thanks very much.

Warranties commonly carry conditions and that is understandable. Take your new Merc to a mechanic who puts in generic spark plugs and you violate the terms of that cover. Fair enough. Makes sense. Gina's case does not appear to make sense. We urge homeowners to check the fine print of assurances very carefully.

Gina is not the only one to tell us about bad building experiences. Unfortunately, there are many unhappy homeowners out there, and many of their complaints relate to finishing. For some reason, Cape Town builders have a reputation as poor finishers. They are fine with the demolition and wet work but when it comes to finishing, they go off the boil. Why? Just because. It doesn't seem to matter if you are paying a contractor per day, so that it is in his or her interest to carry on working. They just don't want to finish. Peter from Constantia said that he eventually took leave and did all the finishing himself – skirting boards and all.

Some hidden costs that don't remain hidden for very long (and expenses that need to be factored into the budget):

- Plumbing, electrical conduits, planning for lights and plugs, TV, computer, phones
- Security/intercom, security gates
- Removing and reinstalling security system
- Telkom lines and computer system
- Removing and reinstalling your entertainment systems, including TV, DVD player, etc, and more if you want cabling to different rooms
- Burglar bars for new windows
- Cleaning materials to clean the windows and mess
- Increased water consumption – when cement gets mixed, taps drip and pipes get hit 'by mistake'
- Endless amounts of rewiring that the electrician will call for – including a new earth spike
- Extra cement, plaster and Cretestone when an extra or different conduit has to be chased into a wall – there is always at least one occasion when this will occur
- Globes for the new lights
- Re-paving of areas damaged during building; re-grassing the garden
- Replacement of glass that gets broken
- New hinges for doors that might get damaged (not cheap – a good set of brass hinges can set you back R150)
- Tea, coffee and refreshments (Gatsbys) for builders
- Take-away meals when you are too tired to cook (all the time)
- Bottles of gin/whisky to calm nerves

Chapter 9:

Bling your own magnet – **a method for sourcing stainless steel**

'In Denmark, the average marriage lasts 11.3 years. This can sometimes feel a lot longer. But in actual fact, you have more chance of celebrating a silver anniversary with your waste bin than your spouse.'

This is according to an advertisement for garbage bins in the October 2005 edition of *Elle* magazine (UK). The ad goes on to suggest that this may be due to the fact that the bin in question – Vipp – is an 'uncomplicated partner': it does not need to be handled with kid gloves (galvanised steel can tolerate anything) and it takes being used – for up to 25 years. The ad concludes by suggesting that this 'marriage of convenience … takes dumping on your partner into new territory.'

Don't worry, I do not have a secret fetish (oy-ya-yoi, can you imagine?). But I did have a question: how do you know, when purchasing a bin or bathroom towel rail or paper-roll holder in your kitchen, that it is the good stuff and won't morph into a rusty eyesore? With all the drek we dump into our bins, how do we keep the bling blinging? The question was answered by Lance Goodale of Victorian Bathrooms in Lansdowne (www.victorianbathrooms.co.za, contact numbers on page 104).

I must digress for a moment to say that I had bought three items from them about three years ago. These accessories – including a shower caddy – are still in pristine condition, shiny with no rust in sight, which is why I returned for more. The salesperson Susan not only remembered me, but called me by my name. This either means I drove her crazy first time round, or that she has an excellent memory. It is nice to be remembered. Not only that, but customers can help themselves to decent filter coffee and peppermints – the soft ones. No G & Ts in this porsie, but they do have an elegant tray with faceted glasses and a decanter of port. It sure takes some of the sting out when you are about to drop a small fortune on stainless steel knick-knacks for your little house in suburbia.

Stainless steel is not cheap. Add up the price tags for the toilet-roll holder and towel rail and it is scary. And we are not yet including kitchen accessories, such as draining boards.

Don't assume that a high price tag always indicates quality. Goodale watched me agonising over which rails to purchase. They were all sleek and shiny, so how can you tell just from looking which one is better? 'You can't,' Lance said. And then he whipped out his magnet.

The magnet test

'You take a magnet. If it does not stick, the metal is probably non-ferrous, which means it will not rust. Mild steel will rust. They chrome-plate everything so you never know if it is made from mild steel by just looking at it. If the magnet doesn't stick, then it is probably made from a category of non-ferrous metals – such as brass, lead and a specific grade of stainless steel.' Victorian Bathrooms manufacture their own accessories using an electroplating system (which we won't go into here), which is export quality.

After that I never left home without my little piece of fridge magnet.

Some salespeople asked me exactly what I was doing. Others nodded their heads and agreed that yes, the magnet test is the way to go when on stainless steel shopping expeditions. If it sticks, it is no good. If it doesn't, then it is the good stuff. Toilet-roll holders at Pick 'n Pay passed. I bought them at R49.99. They look like R200 designer spikes. I was happy.

However, no bins passed. Every single one failed. Some of the rims (the tops) passed, but not the sides. I began to despair of ever finding a bin to service our needs for the next twenty-five years.

I returned to Victorian Bathrooms to look at hooks and discovered that they are agents for Vipp. Very exciting. They had none in stock, but anyway at three grand for a 30-litre bin, I wasn't buying.

What about stainless steel fridges? They fail the magnet test. I was told by a salesperson in a furniture store that white fridges are epoxy-coated, which prevents rusting. Stainless-steel fridges (that is, not epoxy-coated), are 'ionised', which prevents rust. What exactly does this mean? No one could tell me.

The magnet test saved me big time when I was selecting handles for my cupboards. The most expensive ones caught my eye and after tracking down the supplier I was pointed in the direction of the 'stainless steel handles'. Out came the magnet. It stayed on and did not fall off. 'Oops,' apologised the salesperson, 'no, those ones are not stainless steel.' She even admitted that they were not as good quality as the other (cheaper) handles on that board.

Unfortunately, there is a twist to this tale. It is not as easy as simply doing the magnet test as you will see.

I did the magnet trick on my 18/8 stainless steel everyday cutlery and it clung on for dear life. This cutlery was purchased about a year ago from a catering supplier. It has been hard used, in and out of the dishwasher. It is the same cutlery that is used in many upmarket restaurants and hotels, which is why we bought it. I was told that it is 18/8, not 18/10, but that it would be fine and would not rust. So far, it is still looking good. So, how come the 18/8 stainless has not rusted, when my 18/10 teaspoons have yellowed? The latter were purchased elsewhere round about the same time at an upmarket lifestyle store. I became very confused. Stainless steel is everywhere – from kettles, toasters and trays to containers for toothbrushes. It is seductive and expensive. How do we know what we are buying into? (*see 18/8 vs 18/10 debate*).

It was back to Victorian Bathrooms to quiz Lance Goodale. 'It is a complex area,' he concurred. 'Best to call SASSDA (Southern Africa Stainless Steel Development Association) and ask them to explain all the aspects and grades that are available.'

Look out for the logo with balls

SASSDA are the experts. They have a logo – four little balls on a kite shape – that their members should display on their wares. First point of call was their informative website (www.sassda.co.za). Here I learned about austenitic stainless steel, which can become magnetic through processing. The processing increases strength so it is good quality, although the material fails the magnet test. This throws the magnet test into murky water.

I spoke to SASSDA's Cape Town representative Klaus Weber, who confirmed: certain types of cold processing can make the stainless steel magnetic. 'The magnet test is not a good thing for the housewife, ja.' So where to now?

If the product has the SASSDA logo, you are probably okay. But not all members display the logo, and not all stainless manufacturers belong to the association. 'It is like a golf club, you can't force people to join.'

How does the average consumer – or housewife – work out, just from looking at a product, whether it is a good buy? 'She can't. She has to believe the person selling it to her. If you buy wood, you can't always judge if it is oak or another wood, you have to take their word for it. There are certain limits for the housewife. She can't get it analysed.'

In other words, buy from a reputable shop where you have right of return if something goes wrong.

Pickling and passivating is good

An SASSDA pamphlet titled 'Stay Streets ahead with Stainless Steel' explained that stainless is 'essentially a low carbon steel to which chromium has been added. It is this addition of chromium, in amounts greater than approximately 12%, that gives the steel its unique stainless corrosion-resisting properties.' The chromium allows the 'formation of a tough, adherent, invisible, corrosion-resisting chromium oxide film on the surface'. If there is mechanical damage, as long as oxygen is present – even a minuscule amount – the film can regenerate and do a 'self healing' number. Amazing stuff, which means that stainless steel can keep on regenerating its good looks.

If you are into heavy metal on your patio and want to install outdoor furniture, the association recommends that all welds should 'be pickled and passivated after welding'. Pickled and passivated? Uncharted territory that our top chefs might consider exploring.

According to my *South African Concise Oxford Dictionary*, passivated is when 'you make a metal or other substance un-reactive by coating or otherwise

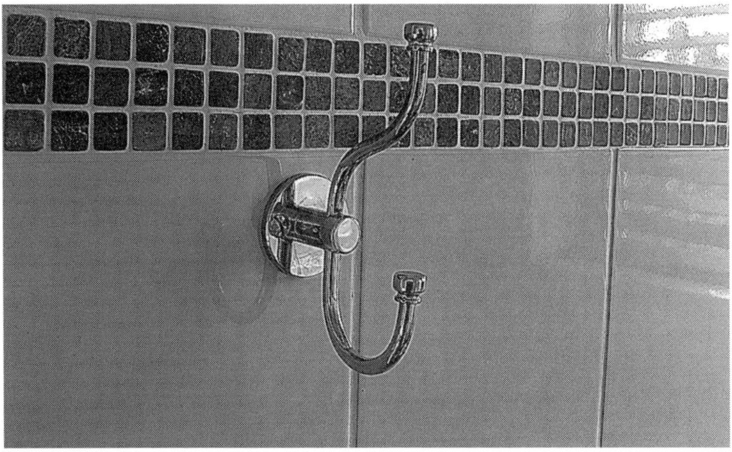

altering its surface'. Pickled: immersing a metal object in an acid solution for cleaning. We all need to watch out for imitations and dodgy imports.

Whether for exterior or interior use, Weber emphasised that stainless needs loving care and must be cleaned properly – and regularly. A homeowner complained to SASSDA that her railing had rusted, but it turned out that it had not been cleaned for eight months. 'If you maintain it, you won't have problems. You have to fall in love with stainless steel,' he murmured, while stroking a garbage bin at @home in Constantia Village. 'In my lectures for SASSDA, I say that stainless is a partner for life. You don't have to marry it but you can have it forever, if you maintain it properly'. Sounds like the Vipp ad.

Wash & wear & seaside care

So how do you give your stainless steel proper loving care? Liquid dishwashing soap is good. Use a soft cloth – stay away from those horrible steel wool pads. If there is a lot of dirt, Handy Andy will do. There are specialist stainless cleaning products that are supposed to bring out the gleam. (SASSDA have a list of recommended products.)

In addition to maintenance, it is important to buy the correct grade of stainless for the context in which you are using it. There are international grading systems to help you do this. 'If you live by the sea and have hand railings, you need to choose the right quality,' Weber says. 'There is marine quality and interior quality. If you are close to the sea, it is best to buy 316 (Marine). For interior, you can go for 304, but if you live close to the sea, 316 may be better inside as well.'

As to what constitutes 'by the sea', that's another issue. Weber mused that when he came to live in Cape Town a decade ago, he considered 300 m away from the beach to be 'by the sea'. After seeing what happens to exterior railings in this city, he has changed his thinking. 'Three kilometres away is still on the beach.' Apparently, our air is 'very aggressive – full of sand, salt and chlorine' and, as all Capetonians know, the south-easter is unforgiving.

Architects and designers should know what grade is best but consumers can call SASSDA, who will refer them to an accredited manufacturer. The same goes for pots, pans and the kitchen sink (they recommend Franke). They will tell anxious housewives and househusbands where to go, so they don't need to rely solely on the magnet test or take to tapping bins as if they are buying a second-hand car. Or you can always sign up for a stainless steel course.

Pickling, schmickling – this whole saga is too much to absorb – something that stainless steel does not do. Perhaps we'll just stay with our trusty Addis plastic bin.

18/8 vs 18/10 – stainless steel cutlery

There are various grades used to describe types of stainless used for cutlery (aka flatware). The two that you will probably hear when shopping are 18/8 and 18/10. The latter is supposed to be superior. The 18 refers to the 18% chromium content. Chromium is the ingredient that gives it strength. If you see 18, that's good. The number that follows it refers to the nickel content. Nickel is the bling component. This is what makes your cutlery shine, and apparently makes it resistant to rusting and staining. 18/10 is theoretically the best you can do. Right? Let's throw in a wild card. We bought 18/8 grade from a supplier who sells to trade – restaurants and hotels. This cutlery has fared much better than the so-called 18/10 canteen we were given as a present a few years ago.

While putting this book together, I came across a website (www.silver-superstore.com) which slices right through the 18/8 vs 18/10 spiel. These numbers are merely 'nicknames' for the lay person, they say, and 'are only used for marketing efforts by flatware manufacturers'. They claim that when manufacturers purchase stainless steel from a steel mill, 'they all purchase stainless steel Grade 304, which has a range of 18–20% chromium, and 8–10% nickel content.' Let's not even go into Grade 304, except to note that, according to the site, Grade 304 in flatware is usually at the lower end of that range. 'To keep the cost down, steel manufacturers will make grade 304 with 8.2% nickel, which clears the legal hurdle of calling it 18/10.' They ask: 'What does all this mean?' They answer: 'It means that there is no difference between 18/8 and 18/10 stainless steel in flatware. The difference between the two is purely a marketing effort.' Other merchants may disagree. And confused consumers, what do we do? Buy from a reputable dealer, so no matter what the classification, if it doesn't keep the bling in the wash, you can ask for a refund.

Chapter 10:

Bathrooms – shopping with an immunity clause

In reality TV shows like *Survivor*, contestants complete tasks in each episode in order to win immunity. Immunity means they cannot be voted off, even if everyone else hates them. I felt like I had immunity when it came to purchasing taps for our bathroom and kitchen. It brought back memories of Sunday window-shopping in the Old South Africa, when no shops were open. You could look but not buy.

During our renovations, Greg reckoned that there was no point in installing a new high-pressure geyser (600KPA). We had a 400KPA (150 litres) geyser, which was good enough for our needs. For a good-quality, decent-sized (200 litre) 600KPA geyser, one is looking at R3000, plus up to R2000 for installation. That was five grand we could spend elsewhere.

You probably need a high-pressure geyser if you have a large home (300 square metres or more), and if the distance from your geyser to your furthest shower point is substantial.

When I had to look for taps for the kitchen, I *platzed* (swooned), doll. I swooned (more *platzing*) when I saw magnificent shiny taps that look like Brancusi sculptures. 'Do you have a high-pressure geyser?' sneered the snooty salesperson, eyeballing me in my bedraggled renovator's state. Nope, I admitted. 'Sorry, you can't have these,' she chirped, adding, 'they are expensive, Ladee.' The price: R5700. I was flooded, to use an apt metaphor, by a mixed wash of emotions: relief and yearning.

Most of the beautiful taps that I have seen are only suitable for a high-pressure geyser. It has really been a case of looking and not acquiring. I thank Greg for his foresight. Taps are what he would classify as décor – a tap is a tap. What is important is that the plumbing is done correctly.

Most people associate the plumber with disasters: a leaking tap or burst pipe. But the plumber has a critical role to play in designing and ensuring that everything flows smoothly and efficiently. Top of the list is to deliver hot water over the shortest possible distance to the areas where water is most frequently required, which is usually the kitchen. It is a simple matter of physics that the water inside the hot-water pipe cools down while the tap is closed. That is why it sometimes takes a minute or two for the hot water to start running through the tap. If you added up how many hundreds of litres of water you wasted waiting for the hot water to arrive, you could irrigate the Karoo. There ought to be a law making it illegal to locate the geyser miles away. But there isn't. Just the fact that, if your plumber plonks the geyser miles from the kitchen, he/she is an idiot. Unfortunately the architect/designer/draughtsperson usually doesn't bother to climb into the roof to see where the geyser is when relocating the kitchen. So get your plumber to give his advice at the planning stage if you are considering a new kitchen and bathroom.

Tip: I have said this before but will say it again: ensure that you take photos of your pipes before you tile and install sanitary ware, otherwise when you drill at a later stage you may hit a pipe.

Can't take the pressure?

The plumber needs to be on site from the foundation stage. Our first plumber, Rudi, went walkabout and never returned. Roderick Wall stepped in and ably got all systems going. Mistakes people commonly make? 'They buy stuff without getting the plumber's advice,' he says. 'For instance, if you install mixers (taps

that mix hot and cold water) you have to install a valve to balance the pressure, so that the pressure from the taps equals the geyser pressure.'

If a new geyser is necessary, get your plumber to include the relocation and/or installation costs in the quote. In most houses, geysers are centrally located. It may, however, make far more sense to put the geyser near the kitchen and install an auxiliary hot-water delivery system near bathrooms. This may save thousands in water and electricity bills. (We didn't need to do this because our shower points and kitchen are close to each other and our house is not huge.)

Talking of water consumption, we bought three new toilets because of the substantial savings represented in a dual-flush mechanism. According to the September 2005 edition of the UK *Kitchens & Bathrooms* magazine, most of us use nine litres of drinking water to flush the toilet, even if that amount is not required for each flush. EU regulations recommend that the maximum flush should be six litres, but this only applies to new WCs. A one-litre saving per flush will save 5800 litres of water per year, based on an average family of four. Most dual-flush loos operate on a six and four litre ratio, but there are units that operate at four and two litres. (There's also that old trick of putting a brick in the cistern – the average brick displaces close to 2 litres of water, which is how much you'd save every time the cistern fills up post flush. Best of all it costs you nothing, especially if you have a few bricks left over after your renovations.)

Next time you brush your teeth, consider this: about eight litres of water is wasted for each minute that a tap is left running; one can reduce this figure by half by installing flow regulators.

Underground movements

A significant part of our bathroom renovation is unseen: we put money into the concealed stuff, like UGs (underground pipes) and regulators.

If you move toilets, you may need to re-route the water supply and drainage (more expense). We were able to put in an extra toilet in the upstairs extension at a minimal cost because there was an existing bathroom below, so supply and waste lines were conveniently close.

Talking about money: do not chop and change your mind about where you want your sanitary ware and sinks moved. You'll pay more every time something is moved, especially near the end once walls have been plastered and tiled.

Set the geyser thermostat at 45 degrees. Most people set it at 60 degrees, which is much too high. This is a point made regularly in the media, but is worth noting again. It will save a fortune on electricity bills, since all you are doing is heating water to a temperature much higher than required. More importantly, the high temperature could also cause accidental scalding, particularly of young children and seniors.

In the kitchen, install ball valves (stopcocks) for the supply to appliances as well as kitchen sinks. This way, when the washing machine starts leaking, it can be turned off without affecting the rest of the house, and repair work can be done without interrupting other parts of the kitchen. We installed our stopcocks below the kitchen counter tops because we don't relish the idea of taps sticking out of the wall, near the working surface. Spoils the décor scheme.

If you are renovating an older house and you have had problems with blocked drains and waste pipes, then use the opportunity, like we did, to re-do those creaking plumbing lines. Your plumbing is only as good as the run-off of your waste pipe. The most expensive toilets on earth will block up if the waste pipes are no good.

Wherever possible, try to avoid 90-degree bends underground, as this is where blockages occur. Try and get the lines straight or at 135 degrees. The one thing plumbers and surgeons have in common is that they can bury their mistakes. Ask your plumber to let you check the UG waste pipes before they are covered up.

Moving our kitchen and adding a shower and toilet wasn't cheap, but it was essential. We used the opportunity to add an outside scullery point in the yard at which we can wash things off, and an outside hot and cold shower point near the pool. We also turned one of the garden taps near our braai into a useful water-supply point.

Sanitary décor

As far as taps and basins were concerned we opted for classic units, white ceramic tiles on the walls, broken up with a listello made from tumbled (i.e. unpolished) mosaic in earthy shades. For the uninitiated, a listello is a decorative border made from ceramic, mosaic or other tiles, with mesh backing for easy application. Purchase prefabricated listellos or you can get your own made up. Not all tile shops are keen on this one as they are labour intensive to produce. It's a nifty way of breaking up a plain wall and visually linking floor and wall by juxtaposing pieces of floor and wall tiles.

Again, here we went with what we like and what we know works for us. After we bought our house, we revamped the family bathroom and went the listello/ceramic white tile route. We were inspired by public amenities where there are a minimum of crevices and traps for dirt and mould to breed. Three years later, the bathroom is in mint condition. We figured we would stay with the scheme – we also like the continuity of having similar finishes in all the bathrooms.

Slippery when wet – bathroom safety

While on the subject of hygiene and surfaces that are easy to maintain, let's take a moment to turn our gaze towards taps. When buying taps, do consider the needs of people who may find it difficult to turn the handles. Smooth, round knobs are a pain if you have arthritis. Children may not be able to work new-fangled contraptions. Never mind that – we saw hideously expensive modernist taps with sharp edges which appeared downright dangerous. Make sure that your pretty tiles are non-slip; that the wooden flooring is splinter-free – and waterproof. You don't want to go into survivor mode, wading through a stinking wet room, just to get to the shower.

Splashing out on wet rooms

Talking of which, if you are sitting with a disposable year-end bonus, you could have loads of fun shopping for the bathroom – or wet rooms, as the trendoids are hankering after. What is the difference between a wet room and a bathroom? No one could tell me exactly. A few bathroom salesmen blushed and started giggling. Then I found the answer in Terrence Conran's *The Ultimate House Book* (Conran Octopus). 'A wet room is not so much fitted, as de-fitted,' he explains, 'with shower heads draining to a sink hole in the floor and all surfaces fully

waterproofed so there is no need for screens or cubicles.' He says that wet rooms make good sense if space is limited, but they can be difficult to construct because everything needs to be waterproofed. Floors have to be sloped correctly so that everything drains out – and not into the rest of the house. Ceilings may also need extra waterproofing.

It is also in vogue to build baths and toilets in the bedroom. It is not my idea of fun to have no privacy while on the loo. It may, of course, thrill honeymooners. Then there's the high-tech hypochondriac version: a Japanese manufacturer has apparently made a toilet with a built-in urine analyser, which can send details of your urine to your doctor.

Beam me to your shower pod

Writers in décor publications abroad are raving about 'shower pods', which come accessorised with a host of luxuries. One model, which sells for about thirty thousand pounds, offers a Scottish shower (alternating hot and cold shower), foot spa, sauna, MP3 player, special lighting and a love seat. Some of the showers are prefabricated, which may bring costs down.

Getting back to earth for those of us working with a bit less than thirty thousand pounds, it is prudent to consider the practicalities of basins for the average family. A gorgeous bowl suspended on glass may look sexy in a guesthouse, but how will it fare when mother and two daughters are engaged in a teeth-brushing session at 6.40 am on a school day? Yikes.

Go into the family bathrooms of your friends and check out how their designer basins are panning out in terms of toothpaste stains. We coveted a lovely stone-finish basin but changed our minds when we saw it in use in a family bathroom; it didn't look very sanitary and the people admitted that the rim was sharp, had nicked their chins, there was no place for soap, and everything dripped onto the vanity.

The unplanned bathroom

It wasn't part of the plan to redo our main bedroom's en suite bathroom, but as the bedroom took on its new look, the bathroom, in shades of mustard, looked sad and forlorn. Okay, it looked hideous in relation to the renovated areas. Our style council in the form of Jessie and Sarah petitioned parents: 'Are you actually going to leave it like this. You can't.' Hard to argue with that. We kept our costs down in that we did not move the bath or toilet. Then again, we didn't have many options in the small room. We would have liked to add a

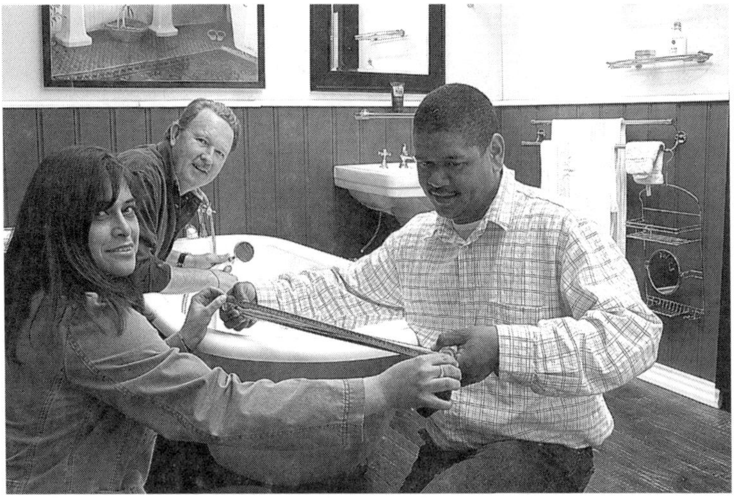

shower, but could not fit one in without a complete re-jig and did not want a half-size bath. We did not want to chuck out the bathtub, just in case one of us wants a soak. (We are definitely shower people and not bath people, but in term of re-sale, tubs are a plus.)

The basin was cracked and had to go, but the bath was pristine on account of the fact that we hardly use it. Baths are relatively cheap (budget priced from R500) but if you add in the cost of the labour to hack the bath out, you can triple that price. Plus the rubble must be schlepped away to the resting place where shards of unwanted baths go.

Recycle – go in for a good spray job

We like the idea of recycling, so we decided to have the bath spray-painted white by Mend-a-Bath (R880 with a 5-year guarantee). Given Nconjane of Mend, who has 13 years' experience in the industry, impressed us with the care he took in taping up all surfaces before spraying. The bath looks good. Although a ceramic bath is cold (you need to warm it up) it is nice and solid – not like the fibreglass bath we were considering, which felt tacky and plasticky.

Even this seemingly easy decision was not easy to execute. There are several companies who spray-paint baths. How do you decide which one to go for? They all sound like they know what they are doing. A friend of a friend of a friend heard about my plight and she kindly invited me over to check out her baths, which she had had sprayed by two different companies, within a short space of time. Bath exhibit A was sprayed by Mend-a-Bath. Bath Exhibit

B was sprayed by another company. The price differential was marginal and both were guaranteed. Five years later and Bath B is cracked and pimply, while Bath A looks as good as new. It is scary. As a consumer, it is very difficult to know which way to turn. Who wants a bath that has a bad case of cellulite? Ask companies for referrals and go and look at how the products have fared. Obviously, you'll have to check that the customers you are referred to are not related to the owners or staff of the shop you are buying from.

Oh, the vanity ...

We were shocked by the prices of off-the-peg vanities which we saw. Design wise, we didn't find one that came close to our needs. You can't exactly call us a family of giants, and yet we find the standard vanity units much too low. You have to stoop as you use the taps. The back hurts. Mike our cupboard man made our bathroom cupboards with legs and fitted clip-on stainless steel kicker plates which can be removed when mopping up wet floors.

Mike also used the same system for our kitchen cupboards. It makes sense. By definition, bathrooms and kitchens are wet places. It's fantastic to be able to remove the kicker plates and dry up the spills. And it's hygienic. It also saves the bases from inevitable wear and tear.

At this point, things were ticking along nicely with the painting. Not as fast as we would have liked, mind you. White Canvas by Plascon was looking neat. To me the paint job was a bit like a good makeup job (as in cosmetics); it gave us an immediate lift. We felt good that the product lived up to the sales talk. When purchasing supplies, it is hard to separate sales pitch from reality. How will the product actually perform?

You have the *phadrus* (regret) factor creeping in. Maybe, you should have gone el cheapo? There are areas that you can take a gamble with, but paint, we were told by everyone, is not something to play with. The Cashmere paint lived up to its rep (translation: 'reputation' in teen talk). It was creamy and, as claimed by the salesperson, it did cover up blemishes and bits of uneven wall. I must add that at the point when we were creaming our walls, we were two weeks past our self-imposed deadline date. We thought we'd be home alone, instead we were watching the builders and painters involved in a territorial squabble which we could not fathom. What I would have done for only one of those shower pods to wash away the renovation anxiety, especially a Scottish shower.

The oops factor …

Oops, the measurements for the upstairs door of the toilet were hopelessly out. A standard door does not fit. There is no place to open or close the thing. Who messed up? Don't ask. The solution: a custom-made concertina door or nothing. Fortunately, a half-wall provides privacy from the road. We'll leave it for now: a toilet with a view. Ja, ja. I know what I said, about a page back about lack of privacy in open-plan bathrooms. Sometimes, us renovators need to go with the flow.

Wasted

Doing this renovation, we were astounded by the absolute waste – not only within the building industry, but generally around us, whether cardboard boxes and expensive Styrofoam packaging dumped by supermarkets (we used these when packing up the house) or discarded fittings.

We liked the idea of recycling the fittings in the house, rather than chucking them away. On this note, we were struck by a major irony: it is very big at the moment to use environmentally friendly products – reclaimed stone and the like. People we know are very proud of the fact that they are using solid hardwood flooring derived from 'sustainable managed timber resources and kiln dried to ISO standards'. Lovely. But, one may ask, whatever happened to their lovely non-sustainable wooden windows, which they replaced with aluminium? Oh, a stash was left on the pavement, others chopped up or sold for a song to a dealer, they mumbled, avoiding eye contact.

There is that fabulous Netstar TV advert set to an evocative soundtrack which depicts all the single socks which get lost in the wash, ending up in some exotic sock island in the middle of nowhere. Imagine all the unwanted doorframes, sinks and toilets which end up trashed beyond the possibility of re-use, in door and sanitary-ware limbo. Perhaps they hold deep and meaningful forums on the aesthetics of a throwaway society and how we are made spiritually bereft from impulsive trashy behaviour.

Tip: Think of recycling or re-using your old bathroom tap in another context (such as an outside shower, or a laundry which guests don't see). With the housing crisis, with so many people desperate for homes, many could benefit from decent fittings – such as taps and door handles – which cost a fortune. A barista in a coffee shop I frequent recently remarked that, although she is grateful for the house she recently obtained, the fixtures are hideous cheapies. They are already cracking. She would love the castaways of the family who threw out all their window frames. Anyone out there want to start a database for homeowners to donate or sell their unwanted doors, window frames and toilets?

Chapter 11:

Kitchen part 1 – **getting the essential ingredients right**

'Your kitchen is not an easy space. It has a funny shape, you know.'

Imagine going to a dress designer and being told: 'Your body is a funny shape.' Thanks a lot. We seek out professionals to make us look gorgeous. Granted, our kitchen presented some challenges, with angles and curves in unexpected places, but it is hardly a NASA space station. Needless to say, we did not have much confidence in Kitchen Company 1, and their quote of almost a hundred grand for wrapped melamine cupboards (see chapter 7) did not thrill us.

Tip: Some kitchen companies charge for quotes and others do not. Check.

Kitchen Company 2 demonstrated how the kitchen might look using a nifty computer program which simulates three dimensions and enables you to 'walk through' the space to see how it will hang together. Their quote, which also included wrapped doors, was about half that of Kitchen Company 1. So far so good. But everything went pear-shaped when Young Designer arrived on site to measure. She was dressed in a too tight T-shirt, lots of bling and teensy embroidered shoes. The builders were delighted. They downed tools and gawked. Comments are not for publication.

We asked Young Designer if the person who was going to fit the kitchen would come on site to take final measurements. 'No, just me,' she replied. Was she making allowances for the tiling, cornices, and skirting boards? No answer. Our confidence levels sagged.

Friends of friends had their kitchen done and the person who measured was not the person who installed. Doors did not line up. Horrible. The person who measured blamed the manufacturer. Manufacturer insisted that the measurements were wrong. In many homes, walls are not perfectly square, with blimps and bends. If the person quoting/measuring has little knowledge of how things will hang together, it can cause complications.

Subbies – whose job is it anyway?

To divert from the kitchen for a moment: we hit this problem when the man who installed our carpets arrived on site with no knowledge of what was required (levels of carpets needed to be lined up with the tiled areas, etc.). He had not been briefed by the man who took the measurements. Quote Man was nowhere to be seen, and didn't answer his cell phone. **Big tip: Ask the people who are quoting: are you going to be doing the job yourself? If not, you need to get your sub-contractor on site beforehand so he/she can see what needs to be done.**

There is nothing wrong with operators using subbies, as they are known in the industry, as long as they are brought into the loop to work as a team with their colleagues.

Plotting and planning with graph paper

Back to the kitchen: if you see that your kitchen person is battling to work out one end of the measuring tape from the other, perhaps it is prudent to get someone else to do the job. Preferably someone who doesn't keep commenting on your kitchen's shape.

'Why don't I do the kitchen,' offered Mike, our cupboard man, sharpening his pencil and taking out a wad of good ol' fashioned graph paper to plot and plan his cabinetry. What about 3D elevations? Mike looked at us wearily. Computer programs are great for projecting the image of kitchen but ultimately the measurements have to be precise and drawings are still the best way to go, he said. Indeed, our kitchen, with a concealed pantry under the stairs and cabinet units of varying dimensions, required bespoke shelving.

During the course of planning the kitchen, I asked everyone three questions: what do you like about your kitchen; what do you hate; what would you change if you could. I was surprised by the answers. People said they would like nicer kitchen tops, cupboards, an upgrade of appliances and/or spouse to share the cooking. In other words, most were essentially happy with the layout and were hankering after cosmetic changes. Top of the pops in terms of irritants in the kitchen: the need for a place for vegetables and a loathing for bins in cupboards.

'There is never anywhere for the veggies,' complained several people. 'They go mouldy and sprout inside the cupboard and make it smell.' Our little red trolley – bought at Pick 'n Pay ten years ago – is low tech but works for us. It is easy to clean and portable. Wheel it to the stove, sink, wherever it is required. We hope the trolley will be happy in its new home – in the pantry.

The garbage bin rears its head, again …

The garbage bin in the cupboard is a big issue. BC (before children), we had a cute little disposal unit from Australia which did its job. Then came the children who could not seem to get their aim right. Sweet wrappers, bits of Marie biscuits ended up in the cupboard. We resorted to a family-size bin strategically placed near the door for easy removal. (Unless you are a chapter-hopping reader, you'll know from chapter 9 why we have separation anxiety with our old plastic bin which is still – *sigh* – with us.)

Try before you buy. At an acquaintance's house we attempted to lift a stainless bin which was overflowing with 30 litres of rubbish. It was very, very heavy. 'Heavy? Nah, who cares,' shrugged the lady of the mansion. 'The maid takes it out.'

Think carefully before purchasing those heavy steel stools and chairs that are in vogue at the moment, cautioned a friend. They may be heavy to move around and may nick and chip the tiled or wooden floors.

The kitchen is a busy place, often used by several people at a time. It needs to be able to function and also look good. Reflect for a moment on the names: designer kitchens, gourmet kitchens. What about a takeaway kitchen? I once knew a couple in Sydney who had no oven, only a tiny microwave for warming up pre-packaged meals, which they considered cooking. They did have a great wine cupboard. Talking of which, our friend Robin Back, whose family owns Fairview Wines in Paarl, quipped that the pantry is nice but it would be nicer if we replaced all the food and expanded the wine rack to fill the entire space. On that theme, missing from our old kitchen was a place to keep a bottle of gin and whisky. Friends sit in the kitchen and that's where they want their drink. In our design, we have included a glass-fronted cabinet which looks out over the dining room – just big enough to hold a few bottles and wine glasses.

Working triangle

As for the general layout, kitchen designers talk about the importance of 'the working triangle'. Design guru Terence Conran puts it well when he explains that the three points correspond – or should correspond – to the three main kitchen activity zones: sink (wet area), fridge (cold) and cooker (hot area – includes griller, microwave, steam oven).

According to the excellent *Kitchens, Bedrooms & Bathrooms* magazine (UK, October 2005), German kitchen-fittings specialist Blum has developed a design concept called Dynamic Space that identifies five main activity zones in the kitchen: food storage; non-consumable storage; cleaning; food prep area; and cooking. Maximising storage within these zones streamlines the kitchen 'and leaves more space for other activities such as eating'.

We have done quite well with the wet and hot areas, which are close to one another. The fridge and pantry form the tip of the triangle, but you need to take a couple of steps to get there. However, this is intentional, as it is accessible from the dining room and is next to the kettle. We do not want our guests to have to walk into our kitchen to a fridge that is next to the sink – and see the dirty dishes. To counteract the need for too much walking up and down, we put in a prep bowl (with cold water only) on the peninsula. Guests can get water without going to the sink and we can wash veggies here and use the peninsula (an island which is attached to a bank of cupboards) as a work surface without having to go to the sink. The prep bowl is near to where our old sink used to be, so there was no expense in having to re-plumb another point here.

Terence Conran points out that it is advisable to have workspaces next to both fridge and cooker. If you stand at the fridge and have nowhere to place your dishes, you waste electricity. Ditto with the oven – you need somewhere to put down those baking trays or that cake both from a safety point of view and to reduce energy wastage.

We got down to the measuring with Mike and his wads of graph paper. It is not just about saying, 'Right, we want cupboards over there,' but also about physically doing a mock-up. Take our peninsula, which links our kitchen and dining room. While plotting out the dimensions *in situ*, we realised that our initial measurements would only allow two people to walk in at a time. We made the peninsula skinnier. We measured and allowed space for legs to go under the overhang of the peninsula. (Nothing worse than having your legs bang up against cupboards.) The overhung cupboards were also trimmed, so that you don't lean forward and head butt a piece of melamine when sitting at the peninsula.

These are small details but important, and don't require a degree in ergonomics. You simply have to place yourself in the space and see if it works.

While the kitchen walls were being plastered, Mike very wisely suggested that we needed to construct a wall on one side of the gas hob. Without the wall, people could bump against the hob and this would not be very safe. This could easily have become another oops situation like the door-less toilet, but with dangerous consequences. Interestingly, none of the fancy kitchen designers had raised the safety issue, which is critical with children, the elderly and those with mobility restraints.

Count your decibels

Another issue which no one raised was the noise level of appliances. According to the *Kitchens, Bedrooms & Bathrooms* magazine, normal conversation is around 60 decibels. In an open-plan kitchen/dining room, a fridge that hums loudly may drown out conversation. There are European Union guidelines regarding noise pollution; no such luck in our neck of the woods. Since our old fridge was dying, we were in the market for a new one. Decibel level? The salesperson at the furniture and appliance shop looked at me blankly. How should she know? No one has ever asked before. If we switch it on, we can listen and hear how loud it is, suggested yours truly. 'Sorry, no listening before buying.' Fridges are generally displayed unplugged. Our purchase, a Bosch, turned out to be the silent type. We got lucky. It may be a good idea to reserve your right to return the item if it turns out to be too loud and brassy.

The detailed catalogue for the extractor fan we were considering included specs for decibel counts. It was just over 60 decibels, but that was at its lowest setting, thank you very much. The setting at which it actually does its job was way too loud. The extraction rate was not great either. We asked around and were amazed at how many people admitted that they never switch the thing on because of the noise. One person conceded that hers is not actually connected. Why have it? 'It looks nice,' she shrugged, not in the least embarrassed. Her unit set her back five grand or so. Still, we thought maybe there is an extractor out there that scores on both extraction and noise pollution.

Extractors igniting

Craig, who installed the LPG gas brilliantly, clinched it when he told us that he is regularly called to figure out why a fire started in a kitchen. Extractors are one of the biggest culprits, he said. The fat collects under the hood, and next thing there is heat and the whole lot ignites. Sometimes the motor from the extractor causes the ignition. We decided to go *au naturel*, with open windows as the extraction method.

We have kept our double eye-level oven, which we installed near the gas hob, with a small 500 mm workspace in between. Wall mounted in a box above that is the microwave, so the hot area is all on one wall.

Ironically, the dishwasher is one of the few disappointments of this renovation. Our old machine needed to retire. Greg's company, Food Safety, supplies industrial dishwashers to many of Cape Town's restaurants and hotels. These babies take 3 minutes to do a very dirty load of up to 20 plates and dishes. And that's the slow cycle. The quick wash is about 50 seconds! They also cut down the number of good wine glasses that get broken when you try to wash them by hand. I desperately wanted one of these modern miracles. Bad news: we don't have three-phase power, and the machines can't be boxed in tightly (under counter) because of the heat they generate from the onboard boiler tank. These are mere quibbles: it is highly recommended for the serious dinner-party giver with space, the requisite power, and for around R15,000; your executive personal caterer/spouse will love you madly.

It was back to the store where we bought our fridge. Greg found that the technical specs for almost all the Bosch dishwashing machines are identical: 2.3 Kw rated element, and a small pump. The wash and rinse systems are the same throughout. All you pay extra for is a few fancy lights, a digital timer system, and a few other gizmos that won't make any significant difference to the washing results.

While on the subject of money, it seems apt that I am telling you about the kitchen in chapter 11. Kitchens are one of the biggest ticket items in renovating. Triple oy. You are going to wish that you had access to the USA Federal 'Chapter 11' bankruptcy protection provisions. Chapter 11 allows corporations to reorganise finances so they can avoid liquidation. Boy, oh boy, you are going to need to juggle your finances for this one.

In praise of the pantry

On one hot summer's day, Jessie, Sarah and I spent four hours measuring up shelves for the pantry, which is a little room located under the concrete stairs. I scribbled the measurements on the wall with a koki.

I measured the cereal boxes, tins of tuna (standard and catering size), tomato sauce, pickles, cold drinks, rice packets, tiny tomato-paste tins, Marmite, peanut butter, jam, small packets of chips, treats for school lunches. I measured the vases that are always lying around and have no place. I measured the flour, the pasta boxes, the bottles of wine; I worked out the dimensions for a wine rack. I even made space for the spare rolls of paper towelling, the serviettes, the paper plates, and the wine barrel we use to make our kosher wine.

Mike the cupboard man drew up his cutting schedule. It took him about two hours and he had all the shelves in place. There's a light and there is even space to dump the children's school bags, and a corner to park the little red trolley which holds the potatoes, onions and butternut. It is the best thing in the world to be able to do an inventory of your supplies at a glance without having to open and close cupboards and not find what you are looking for.

Next to the pantry is the broom cupboard, which is the second-best thing in the whole world. It houses the vacuum cleaner, brooms and all those bits of equipment we used to trip over in the kitchen, BR (before renovation). It is amazing how much one can get out of a tiny space, simply by measuring very carefully. It takes time and effort but it is well worth the slog and won't break the bank.

Lights, action

Apparently, 40-somethings require four times more reading light than do young children. An optometrist told me that it is difficult to generalise and a lot has to do with the individual's genetic makeup and optic health. Efficient task lighting is crucial. There are lots of buzz words used in the lighting industry: ambient lighting, atmospherics, mood lighting. Task lighting is what you need to see what you are doing while chopping up in the kitchen, shaving, cutting your nails. All the rest are there to soften atmosphere, to alter the dynamics of the space – subtly or dramatically.

Discuss your lighting need with your electrician and draw up a lighting plan. With building there is a plan for everything, from plugs to pipes. If there isn't provision for a lighting plan, ask for one.

We streamlined our lighting plan and put in rows of down-lighters, which are recessed into the ceiling. Some of them have swivels, which means they can be angled to spotlight a painting. They are cheap and stylish. Where there is more natural light, we used ordinary cheesecake lamps (another word for lights).

We weren't able to put recessed down-lighters in the kitchen as there is a concrete slab on the ceiling. Well, actually we could have but it would have been a bit of a technical nightmare. No matter, the fluorescent strips we installed behind a 50 mm panel under the top-hung cupboards provide crisp task lighting. When it feels too strident, we need only to switch off the big lights, flick on the mini-fluorescents, and the mood changes completely. At night, the effect is dramatic, and one can switch off the main lights and still find one's way to the microwave or kettle. They also make terrific night-lights.

To supplement the down-lighters, we have portable halogen up-lighters all over the house. These are almost without any glare and are equipped with dimmers. Up-lighters throw the light up and are fantastic if you are working at a computer screen – they cut eyestrain dramatically. They frequently go on special for less than R200 at lighting shops and stores like Game.

Then again, gauging from the nationwide power outages, if the country doesn't shape up soon, we'll be using candles.

Chapter 12:

Kitchen part 2 – **How hard can it get? (the search for resilient surfaces)**

Mothers have a way of fast-tracking renovation decision-making. When told by yours truly that we weren't going to go for the black granite we'd planned for our kitchen tops, mother quipped: 'I'm so relieved. It reminds me of tombstones.' Well, thanks for sharing that, ma – some of our best friends have black granite. It looks fantastic. Needless to say, this was not something we could think of pursuing for our abode – particularly since the kitchen is near the guest room in which my mother stays when visiting us. Imagine the comments every morning about the tombstone décor.

When we began our renovations, black granite for the kitchen bench-tops seemed a good choice. Reasonably priced (in relation to lighter-coloured granites) it is reputed to be the hardest of granites. It is heat resistant and hardwearing. We reckoned that it would look smart juxtaposed with white cabinets. However, as the kitchen began to emerge from the rubble and ruins, we had a re-think. Black would be too heavy for the space, which is wedged between the dining room and guest room.

'Don't buy white granite,' we were warned by Disappointed Hubby and Wife, whom we encountered in a tile shop. 'Wine spills and stains your white granite and that is that.' Another couple told us that two granite slabs in their kitchen are beautiful; another section looks like it has a bad case of varicose veins. It appears that it is essential to go and personally select your granite slabs at the supplier. Not all granites are equal. Some are harder, more resilient.

The other side of the story is the people who have had granite for years and swear by it. My friend Barbara, a caterer, does not treat her kitchen with kid gloves and after 15 years her granite looks like it was put in yesterday.

Other materials besides granite

Concrete screed is in vogue as a cheap and stylish bench-top finish. However, acquaintances are unhappy with how their concrete has weathered. Hairline cracks have appeared; it looks dirty, even though it is not.

Stainless steel is hygienic but can scratch easily. It may look stark and sterile, but can work well in domestic kitchens, particularly if it is combined with warmer material like wood. Marble is fabulous for rolling out dough but as it is a soft material it may crumble and can stain easily. Corian – a synthetic finish made by Du Pont – makes for fabulously seamless countertops. No space for mould to hide.

Wood looks fantastic but may warp and needs to be treated and sealed regularly. 'Yikes, watch out for my yellowwood peninsula,' shrieked my friend, guarding her new kitchen. 'Don't put that glass down without a coaster, it marks.' Huh – isn't the kitchen supposed to be used? Isn't that the point?

Unless you are a mister or missus moneybags, you can't afford to make a mistake with the tops, which eat up a chunk of the kitchen budget. Bamboozled by the choices – and prices – we put the kitchen-top conundrum on the back-burner.

Trafficstone: another attack of Stendhal's

Then, while looking for tiles in Paarden Island's mile of tile shops, we stumbled into Moda Tiles and were confronted by a kitchen of superb proportions, with bench tops in speckled crème Trafficstone. Greg and I had our second attack of Stendhal's syndrome (see chapter 7). We swooned in unison. We had never heard of Trafficstone but we had to have it. It looked like a pointillist painting. A solid mass from the distance but, closer up, subtly textured with dots.

Trafficstone is an engineered stone, also known as a quartz derivative, very tough and hardy, explained Moda's Greg Allin, who referred us to Grisha Stelzmann of Majestic Stone in Blackheath.

Stelzmann is a processor of granite and Trafficstone, which means that he cuts, polishes, seals and installs it. The difference between traffic, granite and other finishes? Trafficstone is harder and more scratch-resistant than granite, but quartz derivatives are less heat-resistant than granite. 'You'll be generally fine. Just don't take a frying pan with hot oil and plonk it down on Traffic,' he says. 'Use a trivet.'

Unlike others in the trade who declare that engineered stone is perfect and maintenance-free, Stelzmann takes a more cautious line. Engineered stone should be sealed when it is installed, and the minute you seal any material – granite included – there is the possibility that the sealant will be eaten away by detergents. Yes, he would advise clients to re-seal Trafficstone, as he would with granite. Time frame? 'Granite – probably every two years. Traffic – difficult to say. Might be okay for five years. It depends on the detergents you use and what has been spilt on it.'

Don't think because the granite looks all shiny and pretty that it's kosher. Generally, processors of granite charge extra for sealing. Stelzmann cautions consumers about looking out for hidden costs. The slabs have been purchased and only then are you asked, 'Oh, by the way, it costs *x* for sealing. It should be sealed – do you want me to do it?'

Stain resistant vs stain proof – a big difference

Stelzmann stresses that sealing makes Trafficstone and granite stain *resistant* and not stain *proof*. There's a big difference in those words. Leave a lemon on your granite for a few days, he muses, and see what happens. He knows: a lemon was left for a week in a concealed spot on his kitchen granite top and it literally ate through the sealant into the granite. The same holds for red wine. He uses an imported sealant from Germany, called Akemi. Some processors do not seal black granite as it is very dense, but Stelzmann recommends that black should also be sealed.

We appreciated his honesty and advice. Many operators in the building industry are only interested in closing the deal. They conveniently neglect to tell their clients about long-term care and maintenance. In fairness, as consumers we do not always want to hear the downside. We like the illusion of perfection.

In pursuit of the perfect kitchen top, I did some research on the Internet. I found out that engineered stone consists of stone chips/powder embedded in resin – or plastic, if you want to be precise (see www.splitlevel.net). According to the site, in 1977 an innovative person, Marcello Toncelli of Treviso, Italy, 'developed a way to make a solid block out of the crumbly rock found throughout Italy's Dolomite Mountain region.' He did this by mixing 94% stone particulate and 6% plastic (usually polyester) to hold it together – plus some undisclosed additives.'

Since then, others have manufactured quartz derivatives (made up of many granites). Glass, marble, aluminium and other materials have also been combined with resins and bonding agents to produce all sorts of fantastic tops, some of which even glow in the dark.

A big plus of engineered stone is that there is consistency of colour. You don't get the varicose effect in unexpected places. Stelzmann uses water-jet cutting processes to precision-carve Trafficstone and granite to achieve curvaceous shapes, which can be a bonus ergonomically and visually. It seems that when it comes to granite versus engineered stone, it comes down to taste: what you like or don't. There are pros and cons to all the materials and a lot has to do with how you look after them.

Don't rush

When we hit the festive season with everything shutting down, the shade of Trafficstone we wanted was out of supply. Stelzmann's suggestion was that we shouldn't rush it, but rather make do with temporary tops until suppliers re-opened. It was great advice. We put in cheap temporary melamine tops using offcuts and saw that we had miscalculated. The hob needed to be shifted slightly over to the one wall, otherwise its heat could scorch the cupboard above. We realised that we required glass shelving so that we can have easy access to spices and condiments while cooking.

Tip: Be patient. In haste, one can make bad decisions. Several people we know ordered furniture while still building and regretted it. Despite measuring, the new acquisitions did not fit.

Our decision to go with Trafficstone was largely emotional. It feels cool and smooth to touch and we had to have it. The truth is that we could have gone for granite and a host of other engineered stone materials. Every installer gives you a different spin. How will it perform in relation to granite? Ask me in ten years and I'll tell you how it has stood the test of time. It looks fantastic and the cherry on the top was seeing the counter top in a busy sushi bar. They told us that they have had their Trafficstone for three years. It looks new. Most encouraging.

Splash backs – the versatility of glass

Bench tops sorted, we moved on to selecting splash backs for behind the hob and cooking areas. More choices: tiles, mosaics, rough-cut stone, stainless steel, porcelain – they all look fabulous. Most are expensive. How will they handle splashes of oil and kitchen mess? The manager of a popular restaurant told me sheepishly that their recent renovation, which entailed replacing the rough-hewn stone tiles (very sexy) with smooth glass tiles, came about because, despite vigorous scrubbing, they could not get the bits of wasabi out of the crevices. An exec chef of another establishment mused that they had enough of using skewers to pick out butternut and tomato paste from the mosaic counter-top. A strip of glass made life a lot easier.

Porcelain – if you don't want to cry about spilt Coke

Porcelain is big overseas and gaining popularity here for everything from splash backs to walls and bench tops. Stelzmann is passionate about this product, which he says is hard-wearing and requires no sealing or special care. The advantage is that the same tiles can be used on bench tops, walls and floors, which gives a unified, co-ordinated look.

We had already purchased our ceramic floor tiles but I must say we were intrigued by what he had to say about the new-age porcelain. He sells the Mirage Granito Ceramico range, which he says is 'eight times harder than marble and three times harder than granite' and resistant against common acids such as vinegar, lemon juice, even Coca-Cola. Oil, wine, and coffee also do not leave irremovable marks. 'In the bathroom, perfumes, creams and nail varnish don't stick to, or stain, the surface. Since porcelain contains no water-proofing chemicals, varnishes or resins, it doesn't give off any gases – even when exposed to flames. It's totally heat-resistant – there are no problems with hot saucepans or lit cigarettes.'

We eventually decided on glass for our splash backs. We had seen a number of bad glass jobs where splash backs were already taking heat strain and fading, but Greg was keen on a tinted glass product (heat and fade resistant) he had seen in Australia.

There are several ways of fusing colour to glass. There is the ceramic paint process, whereby the glass is baked in a kiln. Tile size is limited to smallish pieces as the glass tends to get slumped (edges become round and curl). Some processors put their glass through a process of cold fusion. One operator claimed normal paint is not good enough – the bond is not strong and eventually the paint will flake off. Substances are used to bond the colour to the glass, which apparently prevents this flaking. There's no limit to tile size; go as big as you like.

The glass is not translucent so you don't get to see the adhesive lines peeping through. Choose any colour at the hardware store and it can be mixed with the special glass-bonding agent. The process can be used on toughened glass for behind the hob, for screens, even walls. 'In some thicknesses, glass is as strong as ceramic,' we were told. Obscure glass (with patterns or embossing) provides privacy but still filters light.

Subsequent to our initial research on glass, we encountered others who installed ordinary spray-painted glass five or ten years ago on the cheap and the colour has not faded at all. As of writing, our splash backs are not yet in place as we are still waiting for one cupboard to go in above the hob – where the extractor was supposed to be. Will we go for the expensive, internationally patented cold-fused glass or the cheaper painted jobbie? Haven't decided yet.

We had fantastic service and excellent prices from Glass and Mirror, a small owner/operator nearby who installed the glass in our broken windows (a casualty of moving windows) as well as the new windows upstairs. They also installed mirrors in our cupboards. There are certain jobs you can get away with DIY but mirrors can be tricky. No fun to have a panel crash down while you are gazing at your reflection, and in terms of safety you want to make sure that you have the correct thickness of glass.

The local glaziers told us that spray-painted glass works fine for splash backs, so we may go with them on this one. Their quote for our windows was substantially less than their competitor's. It seemed like a total *metzia* (bargain). We asked them to repeat the price. Were they sure of their numbers? Yes, they were. Was this an SABS-approved material? Yes, it was. They showed us the little logo. The catch? None, that we could see. Sometimes, you get lucky finding contractors who work on a lower mark-up but who do not compromise on workmanship or material. They're a gift. Support them.

Check your hinges and runners

Kitchens are high-usage areas and potentially dangerous places. You will notice very quickly if the hinges are inferior. You may end up with lots of spilt milk when the cupboard next to the fridge comes apart. Ask the company or cabinet-maker what make of hinges and runners they are using and, if possible, request a guarantee. Don't take their word for it. Ask to see the packaging.

Sembel-It is a South African company that has built up a formidable reputation, leaving fly-by-nighters behind. And no, they didn't do my kitchen so I have no vested interest here but I use them as an example of a high-profile national operator. They say on their website that they only use Blum hinges and drawer runners which have a lifetime guarantee. Blum is not cheap but their runners glide and glide and glide. They are so beautiful, you just want to stand there and push the drawer in and out.

Anti-bang thingamajiggies – cheap but effective

You don't always have to go for premium hardware. An example: to stop kitchen cupboard doors from banging against the wood when they swing closed, you can buy expensive fancy contraptions that hiss and shut quietly, or you can go practical with the little plastic translucent rubber discs with adhesive on one side. Slightly smaller than Smarties and available from hardware shops, they don't seem to have a name. Ask for the thingamajiggies and provide a description of what they are and they'll know what you are talking about. Position them either on the door or the frame, it doesn't matter.

Thingamajiggies are also great for protecting walls and wall tiles from being chipped by door handles. If you don't want to have door stoppers/jams, then these work neatly, and are almost invisible. To get the positioning correct, the trick is to stick the thingamajig disc onto the outermost point of the door handle with a tiny piece of Prestik putty – just enough to hold the thingamajig in place. Carefully remove the wax paper over the adhesive of the disc. Now your disc is stuck onto the door handle, with a sticky surface facing out. Gently open the door until the sticky surface of the disc connects to the wall. Push until the disc is firmly stuck to the wall. When you close the door, the thingamajig will be stuck to the wall, exactly where it should be. Remove the sticky putty from the door handle and congratulate yourself on a job brilliantly executed.

Linoleum flooring

The best floor covering, in our opinion, is linoleum. It is soft. Unlike tiles, it is warm to walk on. Drop a glass onto a lino floor and the glass has less chance of shattering than it does on a tiled floor. It lasts and lasts forever, it's easy to clean – wash and wipe and you're done. We lived in Sydney and had a linoleum floor. So, if it is so fantastic, you may ask, why did we go with tiles? Our house is open plan with living areas flowing seamlessly from one area to another. The lino or vinyl (as it is also called) that we saw locally looked like … well, like plastic tablecloths on the floor. In glossy mags, we saw finishes which looked like aluminium sheeting but could not find an equivalent in this country that looked as good. If our kitchen was a distinct small-zoned space, we might well have shelved our aesthetic scruples and gone for this material.

Drawers, hooks, half-shelves and suitcase spaces

You can never have enough. **Drawers:** Install them in kitchen, bedroom, bathroom and office. Saves the back as you don't have to bend right down to see what you have at the back of that bottom shelf of the cupboard. **Hooks:** For gowns, towels, shower caps, jackets, dishcloths, belts – put them everywhere. **Half-shelves:** This is where there is deep shelving, e.g. for towels, but then there is a gap at the back which is doing nothing. Slot in a shelf which is half the depth or even a third of the shelf on which the towels are sitting, so it forms a ledge suspended between the towel shelf and the shelf above. Terrific for facecloths, saucers (space in front for mugs and cups which are tall), etc. **Suitcases:** Measure and make sure they can fit in the closets, otherwise if there is a shortfall of three or four centimetres, your baggage will probably end up dusty under the bed.

Electric plate, gas hob or new age oven?

We ditched the electric hob and switched to gas. For gas installers, suppliers, etc., see www.lpgas.co.za, an informative site, facilitated by the Liquefied Petroleum Gas Association of Southern Africa (LPGASA). Initially, I panicked. The absorption method I previously used in cooking rice on electric plates was a disaster. Gas is very quick. The pan heats immediately and my rice was mushy. In hindsight, I should have juxtaposed two electric plates with four gas plates to give the option of different methods.

Induction hobs are very popular overseas. The pan gets hot – drop a dishcloth on the hob and it doesn't burn. The process relies on magnetic reactions and it is only when the pot makes contact that the heat occurs. Like gas, the heat is immediate. From a safety point of view, there are tremendous advantages. If there is space, it is worth considering the installation of a combo of gas, electric and induction. (My soggy rice crisis ends well. I discovered how to make basmati rice in the microwave. It is even better than my absorption method rice. I am a happy cook again.)

If money is no object, you may want to turf out the old oven and invest in the latest trend: a steam oven. The theory is that fat just drops off, resulting in healthier, less fatty food. There are also ovens which allow you to set different temperatures on different shelves. Bake a cake on one shelf at 180 degrees and roast veggies on another shelf at 200 degrees. Other ovens can be opened during baking and the manufacturers claim that the cake will not flop. Seeing is believing, and I haven't seen it. Fridges are talking to kettles and can, they say, alert homeowners when stocks are running low or food is spoiling. Oy vey, what can we say.

Chapter 13:

Circling your guavas – **cherishing what you have so it looks even better**

'Love your guava,' rave our friends. 'And your apple trees, when did you buy them?' They are genuinely surprised when we tell them that the trees in our new courtyard have always been there. Heck, we are surprised. BR (before renovations), no one noticed the trees. The area outside the kitchen door was not exactly a recreational spot. It was a dump with a rusty Hills Hoist washing line. The braai was on the border of this hideous eyesore. When we entertained, we took it in turns to do guard duty and diverted guests' attention to prettier vistas by the pool. We danced, we sang for our supper. It worked. No one spotted the guavas and apples, except the resident squirrels.

We realised that the dump could be reborn as a courtyard, leading off from the repositioned dining room. The French doors, which were previously in the entrance hall, could be recycled. We would have a very nice extension of the braai area and pool. We didn't realise how nice it would be. As this is the last piece of building we have completed, it seems like a good place to end this book.

But we had to make some final adjustments. We decided to raise the patio level outside the lounge so that our folks wouldn't have a big step down from the lounge to the outdoor area. We could re-use our bricks but we needed the labour. We knew we would have to integrate the courtyard with the patio. An extreme makeover was needed. How were we going to cover up this expanse of sand and complete the transformation? We had run out of money and patience. Tiles were in short supply as it was the Silly Season. You get to a point during renovations when you just couldn't care, and this was that crunch time. You will buy pink paint with purple speckles, do a hip-hop routine on the roof, if that is what it takes to finish. You want to re-enter society again and are tired of hearing yourself repeating the renovator's mantra: 'Sorry, unable to make it to the beach because we are still renovating. We're nearly finished.' Turn up the epidural. Wake me up when the hairdresser arrives. Forgive that diversion into birth matters but there are lots of similarities between these two labours of love.

So there I am standing in the sun *shvitzing.* A pile of bricks on what used to be our beautiful lawn and a huge area of sand levelled out at the correct level for the new patio. Decisions, decisions. Edward from Mitchell's Plain has laid out a few sample patterns – basket weave, cross stitch, herring bone, sosatie spiral, rainbow nation zig-zag, Oy. How about mopani worm swirls? Very popular at the moment. No time for dithering – basket weave looked the best for that area. Proceed. We'll worry about the courtyard area and the guava and apple trees tomorrow. Besides which, we haven't even got bricks for that area. As this was all happening, a friend suggested out of the blue that we put bricks in circles around the trees, to accentuate their forms. Brilliant. Just hold that thought until we get the bricks.

Rent a kibitzer

The moral here is that in addition to listening to mothers, hear what all the *kibitzers* have to say. While it is true that a lot of them will offer useless and really stupid advice, they may be an absolute brick and tell you something that is just perfect. According to the University of Birmingham website, the provenance of the term *kibitzer* may be traced to the chess cafés of central Europe at the beginning of the 20th century: 'a *kibitzer* did not play chess, but watched other people playing, and possibly made comments on their play'. Although by definition a *kibitzer* is someone who breaks your concentration and may make unwanted and sometimes intrusive comments, when you are building you need a pack of *kibitzers* to watch your moves and alert you when you get it wrong. True *kibitzers* mean well. They enjoy watching and only want the best for you. That is why mothers-on-site are the archetypal *kibitzers*. They have your interests at heart. Afterwards, as a peace offering, they make you a chopped herring Gatsby with chicken soup on the side.

Of course, you need to block out the *You Should Have* crowd who are bound

to rev up your *phadrus* (regret) levels. It is like booking for a big musical. You have paid through the nose, looked forward to the show. As the usher is ripping your ticket, someone chirps in your ear that the reviews have been awful. Thanks a lot. There you are with your house nearly finished and a friend offers unsolicited advice: 'Why didn't you build a playroom? You should have used travertine/granite/wooden floors. Yours is only just under 300 square metres. Our house is bigger than yours – 600 squares, so wah wah wah.' No thanks, we don't need your comments.

Finding treasure in your backyard

Back to the paving. Edward did the patio and then went on vacation to visit his family in the Eastern Cape. Desperate to cover up the sand with the south-easter having a bad month, we found a paver listed in the Yellow Pages who could do the courtyard where the trees were. We had no references. This is what you call a *voetstoets* hire. The paver did a superb job with little circles around the trees and straight lines echoing the rectangular space. It seemed so obvious. Why hadn't we thought of this in the beginning? Why had we agonised? Why did we waste so much energy over this little space? Because we had to. To get to those omigod moments you have to go through the road blocks and detours as they do on our favourite TV reality show, *The Amazing Race*.

But sometimes, the simplest solutions are staring you in the face. It is really a matter of stepping back and seeing those trees as trees amidst the rubbish in your back yard. Circle them. Demarcate the shapes and suddenly you have a magical courtyard with Zen-like proportions. Don't ask me to give you the numbers for the Zen-like proportions. Visitors from Japan said it is very Zen, so we'll go with their assessment, which included praise for the bench, purchased on sale at Mica.

To inject a flash of colour, we bought cushions from the locally made Handpainted by Carmel range (www.handpaintedbycarmel.com). Carmel fabrics have been treated with a water-repellent coating and are the ultimate in low-maintenance table dressing, which is why they have been a big export success. No need to get *tzihits* (into a pickle) when it rains or when guests spill their wine. They can get wet.

The courtyard personifies the *gefunene geld* principle. More Yiddish here – roughly translated, it is money that you find along the path. It is an unexpected windfall that gives you pleasure. It is something to just enjoy. And this is exactly what happened with the courtyard. With all the ups and downs that go with building, there are moments of pure pleasure when planned and unplanned things come together.

The courtyard works beautifully and complements the interior living area. We love the flow of the spaces and no longer feel like we have cabin fever when sitting in the lounge. BR, we felt boxed in by walls. Now the bedroom section can be totally closed off from the living space – which we never had before. BR, on more than one occasion we emerged out of the shower, which was adjacent to the front door, to find visitors gawking at us dripping all over the floor. Rather embarrassing.

'You're so clever to have made your bedroom wing totally separate. You were so prescient,' commented a friend, who added, 'Don't you love the word prescient?' I'll tell you a secret: we worried about this aspect of our design. We wondered if it would be too much of a schlep to get to the bedrooms. Entering through the front door, you cannot duck into the bedroom section but have to walk around the corner, through the dining room and lounge and then into the bedroom section. Would this one access point be limiting? The old entrance hall had become another bedroom, so that as an entry point was no longer an option. On one winter's night, Greg and I paced up and down, working ourselves into a tizz as we tried to mark out the space and see if we could do it differently. We only had so many square metres and we had to work within the footprint of the ground floor. Besides a small extension to accommodate the new scullery area, the dimensions of the space were the same. The challenge was how to make it work more effectively.

The thing about driving your renovation is that you cannot pass the buck. It is your responsibility to make it work. You can't blame the designer for not 'letting' you have that extra bathroom or placing your dining room about 5 km from the kitchen. Although, we had a draughtsman draw up our plans, it was essentially our vision. It amazes us how many renovators we know who have grumbled that it has not turned out as they envisaged. 'But, why?' queried yours truly to one, who recently added on an enormous living space/kitchen. 'Isn't that what you wanted?' Yes. However, with all the disruptions, they still have only two toilets and no spare room. Why? 'My architect designed it like that,' she shrugged. The solution? More renovations. It will be the family's third lot.

Sure, we had hairy moments but guess what: we are happy. We may not have always got what we wanted – like double-volume doors or seamless shower screens (way too expensive) but we made sure that we got what we needed.

In fact, dear reader, it has worked spectacularly well. We can shut the door of the bedroom as well as the passage (which leads into the lounge) and we do not hear a thing. We can't hear the TV. We also cannot hear the doorbell. People phone us to say, 'Please open up the door.' For the first time, we can have a nap, while the children have their fun. Interesting how things have changed. When they were little, they snoozed, while we tiptoed around. A small point, but once again it underlies the importance of designing for one's needs – here and now.

Domestic retreat away from hard living downstairs

The upstairs office/library has become everything we hoped for. The books, which used to be everywhere, now have a home on one entire wall with custom-built shelving. Luckily, we had a very patient carpenter who humoured me when I said I'd like to measure the shelves to fit the books. It took us five hours. There's space for novels, art books, recipe books and an oversize shelf for jumbo books that formerly fitted in nowhere. Built-in furniture may lack character as opposed to freestanding pieces. However, from a space conservation aspect, if you build it how you want it and measure and plot and plan, then there is nothing to beat built-ins. One only has to look at caravan and boat designs to see how spaces can be configured to work efficiently.

Not only do the books finally have a home but my daughters and I have our desks all kitted out – as we envisaged. It took us a while to migrate upstairs but now that we are there, we love the dimensions, the balcony and views. Although we still work downstairs on occasion – particularly if it is a cold winter's night – we have a place for our stationery and goods. The dining-room table is no longer an extended workstation. And we don't know how we managed without wireless internet access – the laptop has become our most popular piece of technology.

It is good to be able to break away from the family and enter my own domain. When I was working in the lounge or dining room, someone would always interrupt and ask for help with filling out a notice or wanting a snack. Granted, they can still shout from downstairs and I can hear them, but they tend not to shout too much. I like the fact that I can hear them because I would hate to be working in isolation, cut off from my family. Some people would be appalled by this type of arrangement as they require total seclusion. If you are such a person, build a garden shed with heavy-duty door and sound-proofing or find premises away from home.

Virginia Woolf famously said that in order to write, women require a room of their own. A toilet of one's own is even better. It is no fun trekking down the stairs every time you need to go. The inclusion of a toilet upstairs was an inspired afterthought.

In short – we love our house. I know I am repeating the word love but there is no other way to drive the point home. We adore everything. We even love the mistakes – the tiles that are *skeef*, the cornice that dips in the corner. Master craftspeople often include a flaw to remind us that we are only human and that we can never attain the omnipotent perfection of a higher being. That makes a lot of sense. The odd blimp and rough edge in the kitchen are foils for the slab of engineered stone which fits snug as a bug exactly where it should. When we were in the last stages of finishing, I got rattled at the sight of anything that was less than perfect. 'Just wait until it is painted and tiled and you won't notice,' soothed Greg. He was correct.

Change is never easy and, initially, we all fumbled around in the dark, losing our bearings. This tends to happen in the middle of the night when you go to the toilet, reach for a light switch which is no longer there or bang your head against a wall which used to be an empty entrance hall.

Yes, there was plenty of stress and *tsoris* (aggravation) – particularly building during the great holiday shut-down. Our timing could have been better. However, like natural birth, once it's over, it's over. The pain is no longer there and you have a beautiful house. 'It was horrible, admit it,' prompt my friends. 'Nah, not so bad, really not that bad at all,' smiles yours truly. 'A walk in the park actually.'

APPENDIX:

Contact numbers

Submitting plans in SA's major cities

Johannesburg

Any news about my plans? This is probably one of the most frustrating parts of renovating: the waiting game. You need to know how the plans are doing but you don't want to anger some overworked official with persistent questioning. The very sussed city of Johannesburg has a plan that allows you to *kibitz* as much as you like. No more phoning and trying to get through to numbers that seem to be perpetually engaged. Keep track of your building plans online at www.joburg.org.za and follow the links until you get *to Help/Building Plans* and find Building Plans System (BAS). Type in your stand number, the applicant's name or application number or township name. Very efficient. Need a permit for the demolition of a building? It will cost you R443. Have a yen to erect cellular phone structures and masts? You are looking at R2060 for this permit (tariffs correct at time of going to press). Value of your property? Look at the Valuation Services website. They have slapped a copyright clause on this section, so if you want to find out what it says, you'll have to visit the site.

Building plan application forms may be downloaded. Print, fill in, submit to the Development Planning Department counter on the ground floor of the Metro Centre in Braamfontein. They have phone numbers on the site for everything – progress reports on status of plans, inspectors, etc. Here are two numbers to start with: Tel (011) 407 6217/6058.

Durban

Durbs has a very good city site (www.durban.gov.za) and if you follow the links to eThekwini/Municipality/Planning/Building_Inspectorate, you'll find excellent information about building plan submissions. They also require four forms. The D contingent are nice and transparent in terms of committing how long it will take them to consider your plans: minor building works (up to 5 working days); single dwelling (up to 5 working days); large developments (up to 3 weeks); fast-track approval of a large development (up to 2 weeks). Sounds very fast to us. Think we'll move to Durbs. Nice warm sea to swim in. What a pleasure. The Building Inspectorate Branch is on the 1st floor of the City

Engineers Building, 166 Old Fort Road, Durban, KwaZulu-Natal.
Email buildinsp@cesu.durban.gov.za, Tel (031) 3002195 or call the eThekwini Information Centre 0800 331 011 (toll free)

Cape Town

Sorry, we love Cape Town but their site (www.capetown.gov.za) doesn't come close to the city websites of Joburg and Durban for submission of plans. For example, under the heading 'Property Valuation', they go on a spiel about 'vision' ('to continually improve the effectiveness and efficiency of the City of Cape Town's valuation methodologies, to ensure that all citizens enjoy a fair base for the rating of their properties') and 'mission'. Lovely, but us homeowners want information, not philosophy.

Forms cannot be downloaded but must be collected from the municipality in your area. They're very clear about what they want: 'Plans may not be submitted through the post as they must be walked through the system by the author thereof.' Building Plans fall under six of the administrations. Numbers are provided. The Building Plans Department in the CBD is on the 15th floor, Tower Block, Civic Centre, Hertzog Boulevard, and open to the public from 8.30 am to 12.30 pm. Tel (021) 400 3425.

The National Home Builders Registration Council

The National Home Builders Registration Council (NHBRC) was established in terms of the Housing Consumer Protection Measures Act, 1998 (Act No. 95 of 1998). The Council was established to protect the interest of housing consumers, and to regulate the home-building industry. All home builders, regardless of the size or cost of the homes they build, must be registered with the NHBRC in terms of the law. To register, you should complete the application forms, which are available from the nearest provincial office, and forward these along with all the appropriate documentation and fees, to the same office. Forms may be downloaded from www.nhbrc.org.

NHBRC CAPE	021 914 6570
NHBRC GAUTENG	011 317 0000
NHBRC DURBS	031 277 8400

The NHBRC is responsible for the assessment and approval of building plan applications. Worried about dirty business with the property you have just purchased? Call them on their fraud line 0800 20 36 98 (toll free).

Inspectors at large

The NHBRC Inspectorate unit is responsible for the inspection of building work and it must stack up against regulations as laid down in the National Building Regulations and Building Standards Act. Wherever you are building, make sure that the certified building inspectors pay a visit to your site, at the correct time. No point for example in looking at your trenches when they are filled in. Ask your local municipal building office for info.

A19 inspectorate to check your roof trusses

In terms of the national building regulations, an A19 completion certificate is required for all 'rationally designed roofing systems'.

JOHANNESBURG: Head office for the Institute for Timber Construction (ITC) – Eddie Bock (011) 974 1061 or roof inspection services (011) 658 1022/Victor 083 625 2563/Ken 083 610 0581. The ITC are very clued up. Call them when you hit a stone wall and no one else seems to know what is up.
WESTERN CAPE: A19 inspectorate (021) 918 1890 or ITC representative Graham Butler on (021) 557 6851/083 3418686 or Petrus Smidt (engineer) (021) 914 72 93/083 310 2444.
SOUTHERN CAPE: ITC representative Ian Keevey 082 441 8244.
DURBAN: KZN ITC representative Colin Armstrong (031) 209 2045/083 950 4290 or call Gavin Brown (031) 202 5703 (civil and structural engineers).

E-building – sites we'd like to see

Contractors in the building industry are notorious for not returning calls. They are busy, busy bees and it seems that there are more people who need them than they need us. There you are sitting meditating on your horrible outdoor yard. Suddenly there is an epiphany: this could be an entertaining area with a deck. Hmm, but it's midnight and everyone is closed. You tried to get through to a phone number and it was constantly engaged or the bored receptionist told you unhelpfully that you are welcome to come in and look for yourself. You have got nowhere. Days are full with work commitments and you just can't get one person to give you a quote. You know that you should get three written quotes before starting a renovating project. No one answers their mobile phones. Brilliant Builder who built your friend's house has gone to jail. Other Brilliant Builder has retired. Other highly recommended Brilliant Builder is too busy. You haven't even started and you want to give up but you know the spouse will not let you.

Get onto a website and you may find a contractor who provides an email address. This is promising. If he/she actually replies to your email enquiry, then wow, there is hope – lots of hope. Next step, ask for a written quote. All of this can take place after hours. These are scenes we'd like to see but from our experience e-building has not taken off in this country. It should. DIY enthusiasts and home improvers have time on their hands when businesses are shut down.

EE-yaya: designing within the building envelope EE (energy efficiency)

Want your home to be warm in winter and cool in the summer? Get the building envelope right at design level with good insulation. Several websites (including our own Department of Minerals and Energy (www.dme.gov.za/energy/energy_efficiency.html) and the informative US Department of Energy website (http://www.eere.energy.gov/EE/buildings_envelope.html) define the building envelope as 'everything that separates the interior of the building from the outdoor environment', which includes the doors, windows, walls, foundation, roof, and insulation. As a nation, we're generally not so hot when it comes to EE (energy efficiency), with households consuming approximately 24% of the country's energy (www.dme.gov.za). Become more EE by checking out lighting, thermal insulation, energy management, and energy-saving appliances. There are ways and means of improving EE, which include anything from how the foundations are laid out, to orientation (north-facing), materials (concrete/concrete slabs, storm windows, glazing on windows, clay materials, bricks with straw cores, etc.) and construction. Use a geyser blanket to attain the maximum geyser heat even if there are periods when it is switched off. Lower-flow showerheads and faucet contraptions may reduce hot-water consumption.

If you don't have a ceiling, put one in. Curtains and even blinds will mean that the room is warmer and heaters can be turned down.

Master Builders Associations

NATIONAL: Master Builders South Africa (MBSA) formerly BIFSA, PO Box 1619, Halfway House 1685, 234 Alexandra Avenue, Halfway House, Midrand, Tel (011) 205 9000 • www.mbsa.org.za
GAUTENG: Gauteng Master Builders Association, P.O. Box 4841, Halfway House 1685, Tel (011) 805 6611 • www.gmba.co.za
KZN: KwaZulu Natal Master Builders & Allied Trades Association, P.O. Box 582, Westville 3630, Tel (031) 266 7070 • www.mba-kzn.co.za
WESTERN CAPE: Master Builders Western Cape, 1st floor, Belmont Road, Rondebosch, Tel (021) 685 2625 • www.mbawc.org.za
EASTERN CAPE: East Cape Master Builders Association, P.O. Box 7086, Newton Park 6055, Tel (041) 365 1835 • www.ecmba.org.za

Industry watchdogs

The South African Bureau of Standards is the nation's watchdog keeping an eye on national building regulations, production of bricks, cement and building materials. If a product or service has the SABS logo and is a shocker, give them a buzz at one of the offices listed on their website: www.sabs.co.za.

Online resources

Builders, contractors, supplies

Profinder is endorsed by the Association of South African Quality Surveyors, Design South Africa, the SA Guild of Interior Decorators, the SA Institute of Architects, and other associations. Apparently, you can tell them what you are after – say, revamping the hideous avocado-green bathroom for under twenty grand – and they will point match you with those that can hopefully deliver. I have not used this service but it sounds like a good idea. • www.profinder.co.za
Mica hardware – Lots of stores and growing. Mica hope to have 200–300 stores by 2008 and most are open on Sundays. Excellent service. They know their products. Ask about builders' discounts for bulk purchases. Customer Care Line on 086 112 2118. Mica Support Centre 011 607 3600 or see site for stores in your area. • www.mica.co.za
CTM stores are everywhere, including Australia (Brisbane and Sydney).

Excellent service, and best of all most stores are open on Sundays until 2 pm. They are happy to provide samples that you can take home to see what they look like in situ. Don't be put off snobs who say that CTM wares are too mass market. They carry big ranges to suit all tastes, at very competitive prices. We have found that the same lines were much more expensive elsewhere. A brand is brand, so shop around. For instance, we purchased top-grade white porcelain tiles for our bathrooms and kitchen, which were substantially cheaper than at so-called boutique stores. Ditto, grouting and adhesives are well priced. Their website has got to be one of the best South African DIY sites with advice on tiling, painting, etc. Need to work out how many tiles you require for the new floor and wall? Input the dimensions of the room into CTM's on-line estimator and they'll provide you with an estimate of how much you should buy. They say it is best to remove coverings such as wallpaper, cork, vinyl and textiles. No matter how well bonded they appear, rather not take chances and become unstuck when tiling. Strip everything. Wash with sugar soap and make sure everything is dry before you start tiling. • www.ctm.co.za

Cashbuild claims to be the largest retailer of building materials and associated products, selling directly to cash-paying customers through its 144 stores in southern Africa. Target market: homebuilders, home improvers, contractors, farmers, traders and anyone wanting to purchase quality building materials for cash. • www.cashbuild.co.za

Corobrick say that they are the largest manufacturer, distributor and exporter of bricks and allied building products in Africa. Prices vary considerably so do shop around. Ask for builders' discounts. • www.corobrick.co.za

SA Building website does not charge to list building contractors and suppliers as long as they are South African-based companies. Details for architects, builders, designers, etc. on a small database which will hopefully grow. • www.sabuilding.co.za

Virtual Building Expo is a user-friendly and helpful site with listings and contact details for architects, roofers, granite suppliers, flooring, etc. This is like having access to a renovator's little black book. Unfortunately, it only appears to cover the Cape but with so many people wanting to renovate holiday homes in the Cape, we are including this lovely site. • www.buildingexpo.co.za

SA Institute of Architects – Want a referral? Call the SA Institute of Architects. This is a voluntary association and is open to all architects with a recognised academic qualification, a minimum of 24 months' practical experience and an examination in professional practice. • www.saia.org.za

SA Everything – links to everything and anything – building and otherwise – regional and national contacts. • www.saeverything.co.za

Lighting

Electrical Contractors Association of SA – With offices throughout South Africa, the Association regulates the electrical industry, and 'guarantees to rectify defective work or materials on contracts of up to R10 000 by its members.' Of course, the operative word is 'their members'. A contractor may say that he or she is a member but the membership may have lapsed last week, which means the guarantee falls away. In electrical terms, ten grand is not much, so be careful. They say that their membership comprises approximately 3000 electrical contractors, manufacturers and distributors of electrical components and equipment. Membership consists of over 50% of employers in the industry, which in turn employs over 70% of the industry's employees. That is good news for consumers. The ECA offers ongoing advisory and support services: technical, labour relations, legal, contractual and marketing. Tel (011) 392 0000 and see site for numbers nationally. • www.ecasa.co.za

South African Institute of Electrical Engineers – Battling with a complicated design and getting nowhere with your contractors? Ask the Institute of Electrical Engineers if one of their 6000 members can help. Members are involved in manufacturing, electronics, telecommunications, measurement and control, mining, and power infrastructural services. • www.saiee.org.za

Lighting Warehouse has nine showrooms in Johannesburg, Pretoria and KwaZulu-Natal. • www.lightingwarehouse.co.za

Technology: the wireless house

Dial-A-Nerd has branches in Johannesburg and Cape Town with technicians who do house calls. They will get the wireless network going and teach you how to work the system. Call the hotline 086 146 3737. Charges are, as of going to press, R270 p/hour in Johannesburg (R230 p/hour if you pay immediately), R230 p/hour in Cape Town (flat rate). On top of that add R3.50 per km they bill you to travel from their nearest branch. • www.dialanerd.co.za

Nerds on Site is similar to Dial-A-Nerd with branches here and abroad. Ironically, the website is difficult to navigate. Images of cars (their logo) are whizzing in every direction with flashing testimonials from happy clients. Within this balagan, we couldn't find a phone number for any of their branches. Email your service request and they will hopefully respond. • www.nerdsonsite.co.za

World Wide Worx – South African independent technology research organisation focuses on the Internet, mobile business, telecommunications and information technology (IT). WWW is headed by Arthur Goldstuck, who was one of the first people to see the potential of the Internet revolution. He has written extensively on the cultural aspects of web technology. In his latest publication, The Hitch-hiker's Guide to Going Wireless (2005), he talks users through the terminology of 'high-speed', 'hot spot' and other terms which sound very sci-fi. Read this book before you upgrade your mobile phone or computer. It will bring you up to speed. • www.theworx.biz/wireless

Stainless steel, paint, etc.

Southern Africa Stainless Steel Development Association (SASSDA). Unfortunately not all stainless steel manufacturers belong to this voluntary association and therefore cannot use the stainless steel symbol on their goods. Look out for the logo with the kite with four little balls. To find out more about stainless steel, see their site or call their Gauteng office (011) 803 5610 or Cape Town office (021) 790 3158. • www.sassda.co.za

Plascon paint – Wonderful paint site with estimators on how much paint to buy. Type in the dimensions of a room and out clicks the amount. Download a paint-room visualiser to help you see what the room could be like in bright orange. The full version of this program is sold at hardware shops. Call Plascon's Advisory Service 0860 204060 and ask your questions. Paint technicians do home visits (no charge) and advise how much paint is required and can assist with selection of colours. • www.plascon.co.za

SA Thatchers Association of South Africa – Everything you want to know about thatching as in roofs (not as in Maggie and Mark, her son and ex-Cape Town resident). • www.sa-thatchers.co.za

Mazista tiles – Good range of tiles, listellos and accessories at this tile emporium which has branches nationally. Watch out for specials and stock clearances. • www.mazista.co.za

Bathrooms

Victorian Bathrooms – don't be put off by the name. They don't only stock those sexy, freestanding Victorian bathtubs but also carry a large range of classically styled sanitary ware. They assemble their own range of accessories such as grab rails, which keeps prices down. Check out their bathroom lights. They have stylish numbers which may be safely installed in the actual shower cubicle. Not cheap but this is one area where you cannot take chances. Good website with photos and online shopping, but they haven't included dimensions and prices. Johannesburg (011) 325-5503, Cape Town (021) 704-2340 • www.victorianbathrooms.co.za

Plumblink – branches nationally. Online catalogue with 10 840 items. Unfortunately dimensions are on some of the goods and not others. Some images are good quality and can be zoomed in on for extra viewing, while others are not. No prices, which is a drawback. We have found the trade desk at Plumblink in Cape Town to be excellent. They work out estimates and supply the cabling and doodads. • www.plumblink.co.za

Plumbing Africa is a monthly magazine, published 11 times a year. It is targeted at the owners of plumbing businesses. There's info about PlumbDrain Africa, a bi-annual exhibition and an online directory. • www.plumbingafrica.co.za/plumbdrain.htm

Bathrooms Online – Not a home-brewed site but nonetheless lots of advice, tips and links to other useful sites. For example, they suggest space-saving solutions such as installing a corner bath as apposed to a regulation 170 x 80 cm bath. • www.bathrooms-online.web.com

Kitchens

Sembel-It – known for good-quality work, the company has a proven track record and has outlets or agencies throughout the country. They use the German range Blum for their hinges and drawer contraptions. • www.sembelit.co.za

Dynamic Space planner by Blum – This is Blum's take on how to organise a kitchen. With typical German efficiency, they deal with everything from ergonomics, zoning of spaces to storage and how to get more out of drawers by doing away with divisions. Everything has its place and is accounted for. Believe me, there is no subtext of irony in what I say, only unabashed admiration for this brilliant site, which I came across AR (after renovations). • www.dynamicspace.com (also see www.blum.com)

Poggenpohl kitchens – seriously magnificent German crafted and styled kitchens are now available in South Africa through Alpine German Kitchens in

Cape Town (021) 532 2626. This ultra uber chic brand is 110 years old and with 200 'studios' (their terminology) around the world; their fan base is on the increase. Look at the visuals on Poggenpohl's website and you'll see why. Like the roving Rolls Royce salesperson once remarked: 'if you want to know the price, you can't afford it.' Same goes for the Poggenpohl kitchens. Drool, baby, drool. • www.poggenpohl.de

Easylife Kitchens – manufacturer supplying 22 stores in SA. Clients can buy kitchen installed or go the DIY route and assemble themselves.
• www.easylifekitchens.co.za.

Landscaping

The Association has offices in Gauteng, KwaZulu-Natal and Western Cape. Members strive to provide high standards of water conservation, design, quality and workman-ship through training and certification in accordance with the National Water Supply Regulations Act and SA Qualifications Authority. • www.liasa.co.za

South African Landscapers Institute (SALI) has members all over the country. • www.sali.co.za

Expos, trade and décor shows

The Homemakers Fair expos are held nationally – Johannesburg, Cape Town, Pretoria, Bloemfontein, Port Elizabeth and are linked to the direct response magazine of the same name. According to their website, the magazine is distributed to more than 700 000 homes. Their sister magazine, Home Talk, is apparently distributed to 450 000 homes in Johannesburg and Cape Town. The publications are well laid out and easy to read. There's no attempt to dress them up as anything other than what they are: advertising magazines that work well as an expanded form of the Yellow Pages. If people have budget to advertise, chances are that they have some backing behind them.
• www.homemakersfair.co.za

Decorex SA – hosts décor and design exhibitions in three cities: Durban (March), Cape Town (April) and Johannesburg (August). This expo, attended by over 100 000 consumer and trade visitors across the country, is beautifully presented, with attention to details and design. Attractions include discussion forums such as Decorex Talk Show and initiatives to support SA art and design. For instance, Decorex sponsor an artist in each region who is given national exposure at the shows and also facilitate competitions in association with magazines, such as the Sanlam Young South Africans Thinking Ahead design competition for young talent. Most of the leading SA décor and design magazines such as VISI, Elle Décor, House & Leisure and SA Garden & Home, SA Homeowner, Tuis and Food & Home Entertaining showcase their wares.
• www.decorex.co.za

Décor and home furnishing

Handpainted by Carmel – In their Cape Town workshop, Carmel Stoch and her team hand-paint designs onto bull denim cotton cloth which has been treated with a water resistant coating that repels water, wine and spills. Their signature range is tablecloths but they also do mats, cushion covers, bags, pool loungers, etc. When I got my first Carmel tablecloth I was dubious, as I don't like plastic cloths. These cloths have the properties of plastic but look good. They actually get better with time as they soften from use and lose the initial plastic sheen. Best of all, there's minimal care required – a wipe rather than a wash. Carmel exports all over the world. Any ex-pat kugel worth her salt has a Carmel tablecloth or three to adorn her Sydney or London table. Shop in Johannesburg and factory shop in Cape Town with online shopping. My two favourite designs are on the site – 0313 and 0539 – in ochre tones, these motifs cover a multitude of sins and elevate a dreary plastic table to a higher level. Cushions add colour to patios and courtyards, and Carmel will custom-make according to specifications. • www.handpaintedbycarmel.com

Carrol Boyes Functional Art – this South African guru of functional design exports all over the world and also keeps her prices pegged at the local market. The Pewter Queen, as she is often known, also works in other metals like stainless steel, spun aluminium, and cast aluminium. She still makes the popular cutlery and salad spoons, which are classics, and also does furniture, door knobs and balustrades. There are hundreds of designs in her inventory – stationery sets, tissuebox holders, lamp bases, and salt and pepper grinders. In the market for forks? There is a fork of every type. Do you want BBQ, Chef, Relish, Cake or Gherkin? You still have to select design and the type of box you want them to be presented in. Available at CB shops and other stockists. • www.carrolboyes.co.za

Voetstoots disclaimer

Browsing through certain websites, it interests us how the emphasis is often on members or affiliates and there is surprisingly little mention of consumers – their interests and compensation in the event of non-delivery of goods and services. It is all about what members can do for each other, networking opportunities, sports days, braais. Sure, there are plenty of mission statements espousing ethics, but we can't but feel that associations and professional bodies could be more consumer-friendly.

The writer and publisher cannot be held responsible for any bad outcomes as a result of advice or contacts provided in this book. If you have problems, contact the professional body that the contractor belongs to. If there is no professional body, you can shout at the person who gave you the number. Scrutinise small print very carefully and make sure that the contractor who claims to be a member of an accredited association is actually a paid-up member. Best to check with the association and find out how much they will pay out if things go wrong.